Social
Psychology

SAGE COURSE COMPANIONS
KNOWLEDGE AND SKILLS *for* SUCCESS

Social Psychology

Carol Brown

SAGE Publications
London • Thousand Oaks • New Delhi

SAGE Publications Ltd
1 Oliver's Yard
55 City Road
London EC1Y 1SP

SAGE Publications Inc.
2455 Teller Road
Thousand Oaks, California 91320

SAGE Publications India Pvt Ltd
B-42, Panchsheel Enclave
Post Box 4109
New Delhi 110 017

British Library Cataloguing in Publication data

A catalogue record for this book is available from
the British Library

ISBN-10 1-4129-1840-5   ISBN-13 978-1-4129-1840-4
ISBN-10 1-4129-1841-3 (pbk)   ISBN-13 978-1-4129-1841-1

Library of Congress Control Number available

Typeset by C&M Digitals (P) Ltd., Chennai, India
Printed in Great Britain by Cromwell Press Ltd, Trowbridge, Wilts
Printed on paper from sustainable resources

In memory of Mu Pail and to Carol and Peter Hawkins,
with love and thanks for everything

Contents

<table>
<tr><td>

introduction
</td><td></td></tr>
</table>

Why Use this Course Companion to Social Psychology?

This book is designed to help you succeed on your degree level psychology course. The aim is to provide you with a course companion that gives you a short cut to understanding the basics behind social psychology. It is about helping you to gain the most from your degree level course, pass your examinations in psychology and achieve success in your assignments.

It has been designed and written to provide you, the reader, with an easy-to-navigate guide to the commonly taught curriculum in social psychology, and the ways of thinking and writing that your examiners will be looking for when they start to grade your work.

This companion is not to be used instead of a textbook or wider reading, but rather as a means of memorising content and familiarising oneself with the basics of the discipline when preparing for an examination or planning an assessment essay. This book will help you to structure and organise your thoughts, and will enable you to get the most from your textbooks and the other reading that you will do as part of your course. This companion is designed to point you in the direction of key thinkers and key ideas, and to give you the briefest of introductions to their work and how to put their work in context. It will also point you in the direction of the most important readings and thinkers, and will encourage you to widen your reading and research so as to improve your attainment.

This guide therefore provides you with ways of applying the information that you are familiar with in a practical manner, and is aimed at ensuring that you gain the skills necessary to convey your theoretical/academic material successfully.

As you are still relatively new to the study of psychology you may assume that simply learning the material presented in lectures secures high achievement, but actually the learning and rewriting of information will not gain you top marks. Instead, you need to go beyond simply understanding the material to think critically about the research presented to you. The ability to evaluate theories/studies is the essential skill from which a psychologist derives success.

This course companion will help you to understand the key theories/ studies within social psychology, alongside your notes and wider reading. It will also highlight the skills necessary to pass your modules by providing tips on answering questions and specifying running themes within topics.

How to Use this Book

This companion should be used as a supplement to your textbook and lecture notes. You may want to glance through it quickly, reading it in parallel with your course syllabus and textbook, and note where each topic is covered in both the syllabus and this companion. Ideally, you should have already obtained this book before your course starts, so that you can get a quick overview of each topic before you go into the lecture, but if you didn't do this, all is not lost. The companion will still be equally helpful as a revision guide, and as a way of directing you towards the key thinkers and theories in social psychology.

Part one is about how to think like a social psychologist: it will help you to get into the mindset of the subject and think about it critically. As a bonus, of course, it also means learning how to think like your examiner! Examiners want to see that you can handle the basic concepts of your subject: if you need a quick overview of the background to social psychology, this is the section you will find most useful.

Part two goes into the curriculum in more detail, taking each topic and providing you with the key elements. Again, this does not substitute the deeper coverage you will have had in your lectures and texts, but it does provide a quick revision guide, or a "primer" to use before lectures.

You can also use this book either to give yourself a head start before you begin studying social psychology – in other words, give yourself a preview course – or it can be used as a revision aid or, of course, both. Each section contains the following features:

- **Tips** on handling the information in exams, or reminders of key issues. This will help you to anticipate exam questions, and help you to remember the main points to bring in when answering them.
- **Examples** that are useful for putting theory into a "real world" context and can, of course, be used in exams to illustrate the points you make.

- **Running themes** of the areas that will always be of interest to a social psychologist. You will find that these can almost always be brought into an exam question, and you will be expected to do so.
- Input from **key thinkers** in the field, which will be useful to quote in exams, as well as providing you with the main influences and theories within social psychology.
- Sample **exam questions** with outline **answers**. These should help you to be better prepared for the actual questions, even though they will, of course, be different.
- The **Textbook Guide** is about taking your thinking a stage further by introducing some texts which focus on academic thinking. This will help you to take a broader conceptual view of the topic; on a practical level, this is the type of thinking that moves you from a pass to a first!

Part three is a study guide which will help you to get more from your lectures, to remember more when you are sitting exams, and to write essays.

Following the main text is a glossary of the key terms and list of references.

part one
the basics of social psychology

The overall aim of this section is to familiarise you with the basics of social psychology. It will:

- define social psychology as a topic
- look at social psychology and its related disciplines
- give you a brief history of social psychology
- look briefly at the cultural differences
- introduce the founding figures and their core ideas
- encourage you to think like a social psychologist
- help you to understand the general principles of assessment and expected learning outcomes when studying this area of psychology
- provide tips and examples of the running themes you will find throughout the forthcoming text.

1.1

definition

Social psychology is about understanding individual behaviour in a social context. Baron, Byrne & Suls (1989) define it as "the scientific field that seeks to understand the nature and causes of individual behavior in social situations" (p. 6). It therefore looks at human behaviour as influenced by other people and the context in which this occurs.

> *It is **social** psychology because it looks at the interaction between people.*

Social psychologists therefore deal with the factors that lead us to behave in a given way in the presence of others, and look at the conditions under which certain behaviour/actions and feelings occur. Social psychology is to do with the way these feelings, thoughts, beliefs, intentions and goals are constructed and how such psychological factors, in turn, influence our interactions with others.

> *Behaviour or interaction can be measured objectively (an individual has not placed their own views, preconceived ideas or prejudices on an argument or data collection; it is "value free").*
>
> *Because behaviour can be observed, hypotheses about the possible interaction between factors can be tested and the results/data can be collected and analysed, which gives this area of psychology credibility.*

Topics examined in social psychology include: the self, social cognition, attribution theory, social influence, group processes, prejudice and discrimination, interpersonal processes, aggression and prosocial behaviour.

1.2

social psychology and related disciplines/theories

Cognitive psychology
Sees human beings as information processors, but influences social psychology as processes such as memory, attention and perception can be applied to understanding social behaviour.

Behaviourism
States that behaviour can be shaped by positive, negative or no reinforcement such that desirable behaviour can be produced and undesirable behaviour discouraged.

Evolutionary social psychology
Assumes that behaviour is simply the result of biological/innate factors and that social behaviour occurs because it has helped us to adapt, survive and therefore evolve over time.

Individual psychology
Considers that all psychology focuses on the human mind and behaviour, but social psychology is a specific subsection as it looks at how processes occur in the presence of others/within the social context.

Sociology
Differs from social psychology because it focuses on how groups behave – for example, females, juveniles – and emphasises actions of a collective group rather than looking at the individual psychology of people who make up that group.

Although social psychology draws on the contributions and assumptions of individual, cognitive, behaviourist and evolutionary psychology, and on sociology, it is unique in its consideration of all of theses disciplines when looking at behaviour in a social context

1.3

history of social psychology

In any examination or essay you will be expected to know something about where social psychology comes from. This may simply be a matter of demonstrating a general understanding or not getting your origins muddled, but you may well be asked to write directly on the history of the discipline.

Understanding something of the history of social psychology will be crucial in helping you think like a social psychologist.

Early Influences

Aristotle believed that humans were naturally sociable, a necessity which allows us to live together (an individual centred approach), whilst Plato felt that the state controlled the individual and encouraged social responsibility through social context (a socio-centred approach).

Hegel (1770–1831) introduced the concept that society has inevitable links with the development of the social mind. This led to the idea of a group mind, important in the study of social psychology.

Lazarus & Steinthal wrote about Anglo-European influences in 1860. "Volkerpsychologie" emerged, which focused on the idea of a collective mind. It emphasised the notion that personality develops because of cultural and community influences, especially through language, which is both a social product of the community as well as a means of encouraging particular social thought in the individual. Therefore Wundt (1900–1920) encouraged the methodological study of language and its influence on the social being.

Early Texts

Texts focusing on social psychology first emerged at the start of the 20th century. The first notable book in English was published by McDougall in 1908 (*An Introduction to Social Psychology*), which included chapters on emotion and sentiment, morality, character and religion, quite different to those incorporated in the field today. He believed that social behaviour was innate/instinctive and therefore individual, hence his choice of topics. This belief is not the principle upheld in modern social psychology, however.

Allport's work (1924) underpins current thinking to a greater degree, as he acknowledged that social behaviour results from interactions between people. He also took a methodological approach, discussing actual research and emphasising that the field was one of a "science ... which studies the behaviour of the individual in so far as his behaviour stimulates other individuals, or is itself a reaction to this behaviour" (1924: p. 12). His book also dealt with topics still evident today, such as emotion, conformity and the effects of an audience on others.

Allport's work really did help current thinking develop if we look back to our initial definition at the start of the chapter the emphasis was on the three key concepts of social, behaviour and science.

The first handbook on social psychology was published by Murchison in 1935. Murphy & Murphy (1931/37) produced a book summarising the findings of 1,000 studies in social psychology. A text by Klineberg (1940) looked at the interaction between social context and personality development. By the 1950s a number of texts were available on the subject.

Journal Development

- 1950s – *Journal of Abnormal and Social Psychology*
- 1963 – *Journal of Personality, British Journal of Social and Clinical Psychology*
- 1965 – *Journal of Personality and Social Psychology, Journal of Experimental Social Psychology*
- 1971 – *Journal of Applied Social Psychology, European Journal of Social Psychology*
- 1975 – *Social Psychology Quarterly, Personality and Social Psychology Bulletin*
- 1982 – *Social Cognition*
- 1984 – *Journal of Social and Personal Relationships*
- Others now include: *Personality and Social Psychology Review, Group Processes and Intergroup Relations, Social Cognition and European Review of Social Psychology.*

Early Experiments

There is some disagreement about the first true experiment, but the following are certainly among some of the most important.

Triplett (1898) applied the experimental method to investigate the performance of cyclists and schoolchildren on how the presence of others influences overall performance – thus how individuals are affected and behave in the social context.

By 1935 the study of social norms had developed, looking at how individuals behave according to the rules of society. This was conducted by Sherif (1935b).

Lewin, Lippitt & White then began experimental research into leadership and group processes by 1939, looking at effective work ethics under different styles of leadership.

Later Developments

Much of the key research in social psychology developed following World War II, when people became interested in the behaviour of individuals when grouped together and in social situations. Key studies were carried out in several areas.

Some studies focused on how *attitudes* are formed, changed by the social context and measured to ascertain whether change has occurred. Amongst some of the most famous work in social psychology is that on *obedience* conducted by Milgram in his "electric shock" study, which looked at the role an authority figure plays in shaping behaviour. Similarly, Zimbardo's prison simulation notably demonstrated *conformity* to given roles in the social world.

Wider topics then began to emerge, such as *Social perception, aggression, relationships, decision making, prosocial behaviour* and *attribution*, many of which are central to today's topics and will be discussed throughout this text.

Thus the growth years for social psychology occurred during the decades following the 1940s.

1.4

cultural differences in psychology

As we have seen, social psychology has roots in both European and American academia. Initially influences came from Europe (Volkerpsychologie); however, the rise of fascism in Europe in the 1930s resulted in a shift to American dominance. By the 1950s America aided the restoration of social psychology in Europe, although the ideas still remained largely American.

In 1966 the European Association of Experimental Social Psychology was formed to allow discussion of different cultural ideas and, as seen above, international and European journals began to emerge.

European social psychology tends to focus on intergroup behaviour, social identity and collective phenomena (including social representations).

However, American social psychology tends to be more individualistic, ethnocentric and experimental, focusing on topics such as intergroup relations, social identity and social influence.

1.5

founding figures and their core ideas

Inevitably, much of the discussion in this section concerning the founding figures and their core ideas overlaps with the preceding section detailing the history of the discipline. Core ideas had either a philosophical influence (their ideas and beliefs impacted on thinking about social psychology) or a methodological influence (their ways of working and research studies influenced the development and thinking about social psychology).

Philosophical Influences

The two most important figures concerned with philosophical influences were Hegel and Wundt. They introduced the concept that society has inevitable links with the development of the social mind. This led to the idea of a group mind, important in the study of social psychology.

Wundt – highly encouraged the methodological study of language and its influence on the social being.

Methodological Influences

Allport (1920) – social facilitation
Allport introduced the notion that the presence of others (the social group) can facilitate certain behaviour. It was found that an audience would improve an actor's performance in well learned/easy tasks, but lead to a decrease in performance on newly learned/difficult tasks due to social inhibition.

Bandura, Ross & Ross (1963) – social learning theory
Bandura introduced the notion that behaviour in the social world could be modelled. Three groups of children watched a video where an adult was aggressive towards a "bobo doll", and the adult was either just seen to be doing this, was rewarded by another adult for their behaviour or was punished for it. Children who had seen the adult rewarded were found to be more likely to copy such behaviour.

Festinger, Schachter & Back (1950) – cognitive dissonance
Festinger, Schacter and Back brought the idea that when we hold beliefs, attitudes or cognitions which are different, then we experience dissonance – this is an inconsistency that causes discomfort. We are motivated to reduce this by either changing one of our thoughts, beliefs or attitudes or selectively attending to information which supports one of our beliefs and ignores the other (selective exposure hypothesis). Dissonance occurs when there are difficult choices or decisions, or when people participate in behaviour that is contrary to their attitude. Dissonance is thus brought about by effort justification (when aiming to reach a modest goal), induced compliance (when people are forced to comply contrary to their attitude) and free choice (when weighing up decisions).

Tajfel, Billig, Bundy & Flament (1971) – minimal group paradigm and social identity theory

When divided into artificial (minimal) groups, prejudice results simply from the awareness that there is an "outgroup" (the other group). When boys were asked to allocate points to others (which might be converted to rewards) who were either part of their own group or the outgroup, they displayed a strong ingroup preference. That is, they allocated more points on the set task to boys who they believed to be in the same group as themselves. This can be accounted for by Tajfel & Turner's social identity theory (1979), which states that individuals need to maintain a positive sense of personal and social identity: this is partly achieved by emphasising the desirability of one's own group, focusing on distinctions between other "lesser" groups.

Weiner (1986) – attribution theory

Weiner was interested in the attributions made for experiences of success and failure and introduced the idea that we look for explanations of behaviour in the social world. He believed that these were made based on three areas: locus, which could be internal or external; stability, which is whether the cause is stable or changes over time: and controllability.

Milgram (1963) – shock experiment

Participants were told that they were taking part in a study on learning, but always acted as the teacher when they were then responsible for going over paired associate learning tasks. When the learner (a stooge) got the answer wrong, they were told by Milgram that they had to deliver an electric shock. This did not actually happen, although the participant was unaware of this as they had themselves a sample (real!) shock at the start of the experiment. They were encouraged to increase the voltage given after each incorrect answer up to a maximum voltage, and it was found that all participants gave shocks up to 300v, with 65 per cent reaching the highest level of 450v. It seems that obedience is most likely to occur in an unfamiliar environment and in the presence of an authority figure, especially when covert pressure is put upon people to obey. It is also possible that it occurs because the participant felt that someone other than themselves was responsible for their actions.

Haney, Banks & Zimbardo (1973a) – prison study

Volunteers took part in a simulation where they were randomly assigned the role of a prisoner or guard and taken to a converted university basement resembling a prison environment. There was some basic loss of rights for the prisoners, who were unexpectedly arrested, given a uniform and an identification number (they were therefore deindividuated). The study showed that conformity to social roles occurred as part of the social interaction, as both groups displayed more negative emotions and hostility and dehumanisation became apparent. Prisoners became passive, whilst the guards assumed an active, brutal and dominant role. Although normative and informational social influence had a role to play here, deindividuation/the loss of a sense of identity seemed most likely to lead to conformity.

Both this and Milgram's study introduced the notion of social influence, and the ways in which this could be observed/tested.

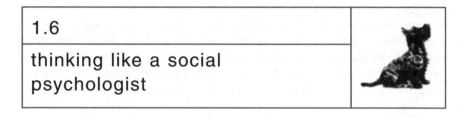

1.6

thinking like a social psychologist

The key to success in your social psychology module is to learn how to think like a social psychologist, including how to speak the language of academic psychology, using their terms and phrases in a relevant way, and understanding how to make links between topics and common themes. This book will give you hints and tips to guide you. It will ensure that you become confident about when and how to use this language and the ways of thinking about the world that come with this language.

The first section introduced some of the basics of social psychology by helping you understand that social psychology involves looking at behaviour in a social context. It also emphasised the notion that this needs to be done in a scientific way, and so to understand truly how to think like a social psychologist you will need first to understand more about this.

The *scientific method* means that you need to test a hypothesis to examine variables that influence behaviour. Thus the hypothesis states that two variables are related in some way and that if you alter one of them, this may cause the participant to alter the other. In psychology we are trying to show that our results are significant and due to the thing we have changed (called the independent variable), rather than due to chance.

In order to think like a social psychologist you therefore need clearly to understand what a hypothesis is and what the role of variables are.

A hypothesis should be a precise, testable statement of a relationship between two or more variables.

There are two types of variables that should be included in each hypothesis. An ***independent variable*** is the thing that the researcher deliberately manipulates, so it is the thing that she purposely changes. A ***dependent variable*** is what one hopes will alter as a result of what is changed (so the DV measures any changes the IV has produced).

Generally, one variable (the IV) is altered to see what effect it has on another variable (the DV). This means that *cause* and *effect* are being measured.

The IV is the thing you are changing.
The DV is the thing you are measuring.

You also need to be aware that your hypothesis can be tested using both experimental and non-experimental methods.

The principle difference is that experiments involve looking at whether manipulating one variable (the IV) has an effect on what you are measuring (the DV) and can involve laboratory experiments or field experiments. For example, in the laboratory the researcher deliberately manipulates variables using standardised procedures (the same method each time), whereas in a field experiment the researcher also deliberately manipulates the IV but does so in the participant's own natural environment.

In contrast, non-experimental methods may be more viable within the social context since, often, studying behaviour in the real world becomes unnatural if transferred to the laboratory and therefore a range of other methods may be required including:

- **Case studies**, which focus on one individual and their behaviour, thoughts, feelings and experiences.
- **Correlations**, which measure the strength of the relationship between two variables; for example, it tests if there is a relationship between two things. It does *not*, however, test cause and effect – so it does not say that one thing causes the other, but simply says there is some relationship between two things.
- **Questionnaires**, which use various types of questions to make a quick and efficient assessment of people's attitudes and which contain fixed or open-ended questions (or both).

- *Observations*, which look at the behaviour of participants in various situations and sees "a relatively unconstrained segment of a persons freely chosen behaviour as it occurs" (Coolican 1990, p. 60). These can be structured or unstructured, but can be carried out in the participant's natural environment.

Such work also needs to be carried out according to ethical guidelines and special note needs to be made of those concerning deception, informed consent, withdrawal, debriefing and protection of participants from harm. When much of the social influence research was originally conducted, the guidelines did not exist and the psychologists conducted their work within a different framework, which subsequent led to consideration being given to the welfare of participants. It is clear from the work of Milgram, Zimbardo and many others that much was learnt about the processes of conformity and obedience; for example, that humans have the potential to obey blindly and follow the instructions of authority figures, or indeed conform to the wider social group. What has been vitally highlighted, therefore, is that psychologists have a double obligation dilemma – to protect and safeguard the wellbeing of their individual participants and to show a responsibility to wider society. Often these two factors may be opposed and you therefore need to consider this when thinking like a social psychologist.

Thinking like a social psychologist involves weighing up the costs and benefits of research to determine if anything valuable will be found for society as a whole by using unethical procedures, or if in fact this is the only way to ensure that knowledge about social behaviour progresses.

Once you understand what social psychology is and how it can be investigated, you are half way to understanding the key principles that underpin this module.

So how do you think like a social psychologist?

You need to focus on how behaviour is influenced by others when interacting with them in the social context. You must consider how an individual behaves, acts or feels in social situations. It is not a discipline that looks at how you behave in a collective way (as a group, such as "students"), but instead takes an individual slant.

To be a successful social psychologist you will need to learn how to consider the theories presented as a scientist, that is, to talk about social behaviour in the context of the research studies. You will also need to be aware that social psychologists use scientific methods when studying people, and that they can test their hypotheses in an experimental or non-experimental way provided that ethical guidelines are always met.

Furthermore, you not only need to understand what social psychology actually is and how to research it, but also require a knowledge of its different types of theories. Each of the following therefore influence the way you might think about this field.

People are not passive in the social situation so you must think about the way cognitive theories apply; for example, the central idea that people use their memory, perception, attention and other means of information processing to interpret and process information about the social situation and others around them.

Since behaviourists believe that our behaviour can be shaped by positive or negative outcomes (reinforcement), then consideration must be given to the way in which the social situation provides this in order to influence behaviour. It is also possible that social behaviour has evolved over time and is an innate response to ensure survival.

> *When studying any topic in social psychology, you need to be aware of how the above theories have influenced their thinking, as this will help you understand their perspective/explanation of behaviour.*
>
> *You must also consider the methodology and the advantages/disadvantages of the methods used, as this will help you evaluate their work.*

1.7	
learning outcomes and assessment	

Learning Outcomes

At the end of your social psychology module you should be able to:

- understand and describe the major theories and areas of research in social psychology
- think critically about the key studies/theories

- understand and be able to evaluate the methods used to research social psychology
- relate the theories and thinking of social psychologists to contemporary social issues
- discuss the contribution that social psychology makes to understanding the individual, the social context and the relationship between the two
- understand the basic history and development of social psychology
- understand the relationship between social psychology and other psychological approaches.

Assessment

You will be assessed in a number of ways, including essay writing, projects and discussion work. Put simply, there are two basic skills that you need to be a good psychologist, and it is these that your examiners will be looking for when assessing you:

- Your **knowledge and understanding** of psychological theories, concepts and studies: to demonstrate this you might give a definition of a psychological term, outline a theory or a particular study carried out.
- Your **evaluation** of a psychological theory/argument/study: this essentially requires you to say what is good or bad about a theory/argument/study and focuses on *how* a theory or idea can be supported by research and *how* it can be criticised by research.

If you simply write out the relevant study and state that it does support/ criticise a theory, you will not gain marks. Your essay questions test more than your ability to memorise and rewrite information. Rather, you are expected to show that you have considered both sides of an argument and are able to draw an overall conclusion – you therefore explicitly need to show *how* a piece of evidence supports or criticises a theory/idea. It is the "why" that will gain you the higher marks, both on this particular question and the paper generally. Put bluntly, this skill demonstrated in your answer is the single factor that will make a difference to achieving the lower or higher grades in your psychology degree.

With regard to achieving the degree you are aiming for, the following broad criteria should apply:

- **70+ marks will give you a first class honours degree** whereby you show a clear, coherent and logical argument that (most importantly) shows an excellent demonstration of the key arguments, concepts and studies and an ability critically to evaluate these. Such analysis needs to reflect original thought, must be related to the set question and must be well supported by scientific evidence gained by the application of your wider reading.

- **60–69 marks will give you an upper second class honours degree** and will require that you show a clear, coherent and logical argument with good performance in the areas above. The main difference here is that you display less originality of thought than of that required for a first class honours. So you will show a good grasp of concepts, the relationship between them, and support your arguments accordingly with the application of wider reading.
- **50–59 marks will give you a lower second class degree**, which means that you demonstrate an organised argument but one that has irrelevant material or omissions, with a general grasp of concepts and logical argument shown. Content may not be directly related to the question and evaluations do not reflect original analysis. There is less evidence of wider reading.
- **40–49 marks would result in a third class degree**, whereby you show a basic understanding of the main concepts and arguments in social psychology but there are errors or omissions and debate may be unstructured and irrelevant. There would also be little evidence of original thought, little use of scientific evidence to support arguments and little evidence of wider reading.

As you can see from these criteria, some of the key skills you require in psychology are an important feature of this text. However, remember that this book is not a replacement for the wider reading you need to gain top marks – it will simply supplement what you know.

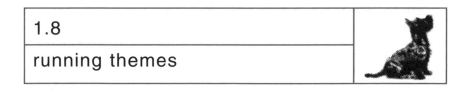

1.8	
running themes	

There will be a number of common themes that will run throughout this book – no matter what topic you are studying, these "running themes" will recur and it is important that you bear these in mind, mention them when appropriate and think about how they make an impact on the topic you are studying:

- ***Compliance***: although a person may privately maintain their own view, they will publicly display the attitudes or behaviour of the majority because they want to be accepted as part of that group and have a desire to be liked (normative social influence).

- **Identification**: when membership of a group is important to a person in the social setting, then they adopt the value of the majority both publicly and privately, although this changes once the particular group is no longer of importance.
- **Internalisation**: views of the social group are internalised and the behaviour/attitudes of the majority are consistent both publicly and privately.
- **Majority social influence**: people change their behaviour so that they adopt that of the majority. People are most likely to conform because they have a desire to be liked and a desire to be right (normative and informational social influence) and so publicly (although not necessarily privately) display the attitudes and behaviours of the dominant group.
- **Minority influence**: when a minority presents a consistent argument, they may be able to influence the attitudes and behaviour of the majority.
- **Social influence**: where people are influenced by others such that they try to display the attitude or behaviour of the social group either by obeying or conforming to the majority or the minority. Social influence occurs because of the desire to be liked and the desire to be right (normative and informational social influence).
- **Normative social influence**: people have the desire to be liked by the social group and therefore conform to the behaviour and attitudes displayed by the majority.
- **Informational social influence**: people will yield to the majority social influence because they want to be accepted and therefore feel the need to be right/display the correct answer or behaviour in order to gain such acceptance.
- **Collective mind**: the idea that individuals form a "collective" or group mind derived from social norms/the social context.
- **Individual centred approach**: the study of social behaviour that emphasises individual experience/behaviour.
- **Socio-centred approach**: the study of behaviour that emphasises the function and structure of the social context.
- **Social norms**: look at how individuals behave according to the rules of society.
- **Deindividuation**: the individual relinquishes individual responsibility for actions and sees behaviour as a consequence of group norms and expectations.

These running themes will help you when using your textbooks as they underpin most topics in the syllabus and will help you to understand that there is common ground between these topics. When revising material, these themes will also provide you with a way of linking your ideas together and in building up a picture of how social psychology applies to the real world. For example, the rules of society (see social norms) underpin all aspects of social behaviour and we are inevitably subject to social influence, particularly the processes of compliance, identification, internalisation and majority social influence. As you will see throughout this book such themes can be involved in a whole range of processes, for example, in the construction of self, the attributions we make, prejudice and discrimination to list just a few. At the start of each chapter the themes most important to the topic are listed, and in some cases expanded upon to give you some indication of the lines along which you could develop your thinking in relation to the material you will gain from your texts and indeed the chapters themselves. Expanding upon these when writing your essays will ensure that you engage on a level of critical thinking that is vital if you want to gain the higher marks.

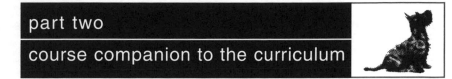

part two

course companion to the curriculum

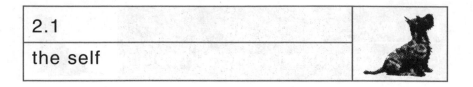

2.1

the self

Core Areas

- Actual, ideal and ought selves
- Collective identity
- Group-based social identity
- Individual versus collective self
- Person-based social identity
- Psychodynamic self
- Relational social identity
- Self-categorisation theory

- Self-maintenance model
- Self motives
- Self-perception theory
- Self-presentation
- Social comparison theory
- Structural and normative fit
- Symbolic interactionalist self

Learning Outcomes

By the end of this chapter you should be able to:

- define and understand the key concepts outlined above;
- describe and evaluate the theories of the key thinkers on self-knowledge;
- understand that there are different types of self;
- examine the concept of social identity and to understand the relationship between the self and group membership;
- look at the different types of self-motives; and
- describe the self-enhancing triad, individual and cultural differences in the self and methods of self-presentation.

Running Themes

- Compliance
- Identification
- Internalisation
- Majority social influence
- Social influence

- Normative social influence
- Informational social influence
- Collective mind
- Individual centred approach
- Deindividuation

Introduction

According to Duval & Wicklund (1972) self-awareness is "a state where you are aware of yourself".

> *Carver and Scheier (1981) distinguish between the private self, which is made up of private thoughts, feelings and attitudes, and the public self, which focuses on public appearance and how others see you.*

Historically the self has been viewed in various ways:

- *Psychodynamic self*: here the self can only be discovered by psychoanalysis where repressed thoughts are brought into the open. The self tries to maintain a balance between infantile desires (the id) and moral reasoning (the superego) to achieve a state of balance (ego).
- *Individual versus collective self*: the individual self has personal and private views and individuals act together and may share an identity. The collective self derives from the group. According to Wundt (1916), the collective self emerges from shared language, customs and so on, and individuals cannot therefore be viewed in isolation. Individuals together therefore form a "group mind".
- *Symbolic interactionalist self*: self emerges as a result of social interaction and the shared meanings and methods of communication (verbal and nonverbal) that result from this. According to Mead's "looking glass self" (1934), our own concept of the self is also derived from seeing ourselves as others see us. Therefore the self emerges as a reflection of society.

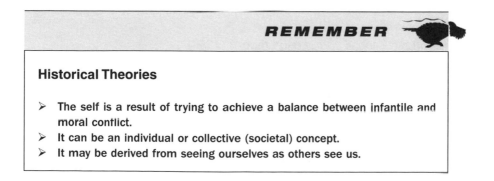

REMEMBER

Historical Theories

➢ The self is a result of trying to achieve a balance between infantile and moral conflict.
➢ It can be an individual or collective (societal) concept.
➢ It may be derived from seeing ourselves as others see us.

> *We can see that this topic covers both the idea that individuals form a "collective" or group mind/sense of self, derived from social norms/the social context, as well as an individual centred approach as it emphasises individual experience/behaviour, for example, the individual self.*

Key Thinkers

Self-knowledge refers to what we know about ourselves, and who we are. Important aspects of the self are stored as self-schemas, that is, a cognitive building block of knowledge containing information about personal attributes.

Higgins (1987)
Identifies three types of self schema: actual self – how we are now; ideal self – how we would like to be; and "ought" self – how we think we should be. The last two are simply guides and according to Higgins's self-discrepancy theory, the self will be motivated to change when there is a discrepancy or difference between the actual self and the ideal or ought selves.

Bem's self-perception theory (1967, 1972)
Proposes that we derive knowledge about the self from the attributions we make about our own behaviour. It can also be derived from imagining ourselves behaving in a given way. This concept of the self is important in motivating behaviour because performance will be impaired if there is an obviously external cause for it, otherwise an over-justification effect occurs whereby motivation increases as behaviour is instead seen as a result of internal factors such as commitment.

Festinger's social comparison theory (1954)
Asserts that the self is derived from social comparisons where our feelings, thoughts and behaviours are compared to (often similar) others such that a social identity and sense of self emerges.

Tesser's self-maintenance model (1988)
Shows that since making upward social comparisons can decrease self concept (not feeling good enough), then people may try to ignore their

similarity to another person or withdraw from a relationship to maintain a positive self-evaluation.

Turner, Hogg, Oakes, Reicher & Wetherall
self-categorisation theory (1987)
Finds that knowledge of the self is also derived from group membership, which produces a sense of social identity. Group membership encourages behaviour to be attributed to the self and "ingroup".

Types of Self and Identity

Different theories have been proposed, but most agree that there is a *social identity*, where the self is seen in terms of group membership, and a *personal identity*, where the self is seen as a result of personal relationships and traits.

Brewer & Gardner (1996) identify three types of self: *the individual self*, based on individual traits; the *relation self*, where it is seen in terms of relationships with others; and the *collective self*, where it is viewed in terms of collective group membership (of one group against another).

Brewer (2001) identified four types:

- *person-based social identity* – where personal identity is based on factors internalised from group membership;
- *relational social identity* – the self is defined from interactions with specific others;
- *group-based social identity* – the self is based on group membership; and
- *collective identity* – the self is seen collectively as part of shared views of a group and their actions.

It is generally agreed that we have multiple selves, depending on the context, but with a degree of integration between them.

Social Identity

The social identity approach looks at the relationship between the self and group membership. Available schemas are used to categorise others and are based on prototypes (typical associations), which leads to a perceived difference between groups. Sometimes these prototypes and categorisation of the average group member fit together (structural fit) and explains behaviour (normative fit), in which case the categorisation used is said to be psychologically salient. In this case individuals may feel depersonalised (loose their sense of personal identity), or the self-fulfilling prophecy may come into play where they start to behave as the categorisation would anticipate. In contrast, membership of positive groups enhance self-esteem.

Self Motives

Motives are important because they aid self-knowledge. There are two classes: validity and consistency, and favourability.

Validity and consistency is where one wants to achieve accurate or valid information about themselves so self-assessment motives and a self-verification process are involved, where people try to ascertain information telling them what sort of person they are and then find consistent evidence to support this. Sedikides (1993) found that self-assessment is strongest in peripheral rather than core aspects of the self, but self-verification is more involved with core aspects.

Favourability is when people have a self-enhancement motive where they try to see themselves in a favourable way. Evidence of this is seen in Steele's self-affirmation theory (1988), where people bring to public attention their positive attributes, especially when they have been viewed less favourably by others. Reflecting on more positive aspects of the self will lead to confirming further positive aspects. Overall, the self-enhancement motive was found to be the strongest.

> *Motives exist to ensure that we understand ourselves better, and to do this we have to find out what we know about ourselves and find consistent and positive evidence to support this.*

Self-esteem

Self-esteem is based on the feelings one has about themselves and the evaluations they make. It is closely linked to social identity, as identification with a group and its societal connotations impacts on self-concept.

Taylor & Brown (1988) found that people either overestimate their good points, overestimate their control of events or are unrealistically optimistic. This is called the self-enhancing triad (Sedikides & Gregg, 2003). Failures, inconsistencies (unexpected positive or negative events) and stressors can all threaten self-esteem and lead to illness. People cope with these by trying to escape, using denial, attacking the threat, downplaying it or expressing concerns (Hogg & Vaughan, 2005).

Individual and Cultural Differences

It has been found that generally self-esteem varies from moderate to very high and there is little evidence to support the popular misconception that low self-esteem accounts for psychological and physical problems and social issues such as delinquency.

Campbell (1990) asserted some differences between individuals and postulated that those with higher self-esteem have more stability and less self-concept confusion and also tend to be more motivated as they recognise success, whereas people with lower self-esteem tend to experience confusion and try to protect themselves by avoiding failure.

Whilst Western cultures are defined as individualistic, others such as Asia, South America and Africa are viewed as collectivist. In terms of the self, individualistic cultures focus on the individual self which is seen as separate, whereas collectivist cultures regard the self as interdependent and connected to the relationships with other people (Markus & Kityama, 1991). Ethnic and racial identity is therefore a significant source of self-esteem mediated by social identity.

REMEMBER

Individual and Cultural Differences

➤ There will be differences in the behaviour of individuals who have low, moderate and high self-esteem, and ethnic and racial identity may also affect feelings about the self.

Self-presentation

Impression management is used to ensure that we create a good impression of ourselves. Usually we act deliberately to ensure that we give a favourable impression of ourselves. Jones & Pittman (1982, in Hogg and Vaughan, 2005) say that this can be done by using self-promotion (assure confidence), ingratiation (getting others to like you), intimidation, exemplification (portray yourself as morally respectable) and supplication (getting others to take pity on you).

Tasks

1 Write down a list of 15 characteristics that you feel best describe you. Using the information provided in this chapter, record which types of self these are and why (for example, are they individual or collectivist?). This will help you to distinguish between the different types on a personal level.

2 Using your textbook, look up one piece of research that supports the view that there are individual differences in the self, and at least one piece of research that shows there are cultural differences. Say *how* each piece of research supports the view that there are differences.

3 Now use your books to write a list of problems while assuming that there are individual and cultural differences and say exactly *why* each point you make is a criticism.

" Compare and contrast theories of the self. "

This question requires you to do more than simply rewrite each of the theories. Instead it asks you to specifically compare (say what is similar) and contrast (say what is different) about each of the theories. You could consider, for example, the emphasis on social rather than individual factors or the explicit role of cognitions. You must ensure that you refer the question back to research evidence, for example, studies and not just simply write out a narrative on each one.

" To what extent has research indicated individual and cultural differences in the self? "

Tasks 2 and 3 above are directly geared towards completion of this essay. You need to use the research you have done for these to answer this question. This chapter provides you with enough information to write a brief introduction, but you then need to use your studies to show where a direct link has been provided between individual and cultural differences and the self and if this is valid or whether, and how, such a link can be criticised.

Common Pitfalls

- The concepts in this chapter are often similar but do have different meanings – you must ensure that you are familiar with each term and theory to avoid confusion in an essay.
- It is all too easy to see individual and cultural differences as a minor area in this topic and to concentrate only on the theories. The tasks above are there to prevent you from doing this, as it is an important and up-and-coming area.
- Remember that it is not sufficient just to know the research evidence in this topic; you also need to be able critically to evaluate it by saying where it can support or criticise your area of discussion.

Textbook guide

BAUMEISTER, R. F. (ED.) (1999). *The self in social psychology*. Philadelphia, PA: Psychology Press. This is an excellent book for providing specific research studies on this area as well as a general background introduction to the topic.

BEM, D. J. (1967). Self perception: An alternative interpretation of cognitive dissonance. *Psychological Review, 74*, 183–200. The original paper looking at this theory.

FESTINGER, L. (1954). A theory of social comparison. *Human Relations,* 117–140. Further background on social comparison theory.

2.2	
social cognition	

Core Areas

- Category
- Cognitive algebra model
- Configuration model
- Heuristics: availability, representiveness, anchoring and adjustment and similarity
- Person memory
- Prototype

- Schema
- Self-categorisation theory
- Self-identity theory
- Social cognition
- Social encoding
- Social Inference
- Social representations

Learning Outcomes

By the end of this chapter you should be able to:

- define the key terms outlined above;
- show an understanding of the processes involved in social cognition and the biases that operate;
- describe and evaluate the work of the key thinkers in this area;
- understand the nature of categories, prototypes and schemas, their use and development;
- define and outline the processes involved in social cognition;
- look at the role of person memory; and
- understand social inference, top-down and bottom-up processing and the types of errors that can occur.

Running Themes

- Compliance
- Social influence
- Normative social influence
- Informational social influence

- Individual centred approach
- Socio-centred approach
- Social norms

Introduction

Social cognition looks at the reciprocal interaction between the social world and mental/cognitive processes. Social representations are the belief systems that simplify the social world by introducing a shared social reality, guiding social action.

> *Social cognition forms a link between cognitive and social psychology.*

Stages of Social Cognition

Generic knowledge
Is based on categories where groups of objects are thought about and perceived in a similar way, and stereotypes, which are based on shared

beliefs. May be represented as prototypes or scripts (routines for particular actions, knowledge, beliefs or events). This links back to Asch's configuration model – the idea of both central traits and the primacy-recency effect.

Perception and attention
Offer limited capacity for information. To gain attention something must be distinctive and salient (distinctive within its context to allow perception and attention), and/or unexpected or relevant to us.

Encoding and interpretation
Means that once perceived, information needs to be encoded. Categories must be accessed – first the most frequent ones (primacy effect), as they have been used most recently.

Organisation
Whereby information is organised by categories.

Relating information to prior knowledge
Where inconsistent or unexpected information is recalled better than consistent, expected information as it is processed more deeply/elaborated upon. This is not, however, relevant to group processes as it is harder to process many inconsistencies about groups, although information consistent with prior knowledge has a strong impact as it is derived from existing knowledge.

Judgements
Four types can be made using heuristics, which are decision rules used to make a judgement/form an attitude, so use mental shortcuts/cues available from memory:

1 **Availability heuristic**: makes judgements about predicted events and behaviour as they are easily available in memory.

2 **Representativeness heuristic**: if an event/behaviour is probable, then this is used to make a social judgment.

3 **Anchoring and adjustment heuristic**: use a starting value on which to base judgements.

4 **Similarity heuristic**: if events/behaviour can be imagined, then it forms a social judgement as already 'simulated'.

REMEMBER

The Processes in Social Cognition

Social cognition involves:

➤ Using categories of knowledge
➤ Perceiving and attending to it
➤ Coding and interpreting it
➤ Organising it
➤ Relating it to prior knowledge
➤ Making judgements using mental shortcuts (heuristics)

Biases in Social Cognition

Primacy/recency effect
When Asch (1946) gave lists of characteristics (first positive then negative), the order was found to be important as the first and last traits were best remembered and given more importance than the middle items. Most notably, if positive items were presented first, they created a more favourable impression of the person.

Positive and negative biases
If no information is given on a person we form a positive impression, but if negative information is provided this forms more of an impression because such information is distinctive or poses danger.

Personal construct and implicit personality theory
Personal ways of categorising and exploring other people simplifies our impression of others.

Physical appearance
This influences impressions, possibly due to the primacy effect. We tend to make generalisations, such as people who are thin are "good" and people who are large are "bad".

Stereotypes
These are used to categorise people, are slow to change, are acquired at an early age, evident in situations of conflict and help make sense of the world.

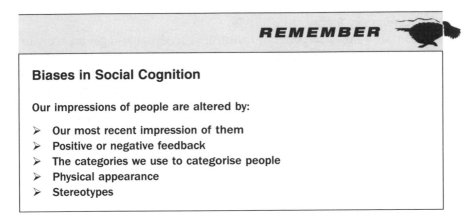

REMEMBER

Biases in Social Cognition

Our impressions of people are altered by:

➤ Our most recent impression of them
➤ Positive or negative feedback
➤ The categories we use to categorise people
➤ Physical appearance
➤ Stereotypes

Key Thinkers

Asch's configuration model (1946)
Demonstrates that when forming an impression of others we focus on key factors/pieces of information called "central traits", and these are very important in forming a final impression of people. The halo effect occurs when one positive attribute leads to perception of others (and the same for negative traits). Less important aspects (peripheral traits) are also involved, but are less significant, in this process.

Anderson's cognitive algebra theory (1965, 1978, 1981)
Suggests that impressions of people are formed by combining pieces of information about a person to complete a whole picture. This approach looks at how information that is positive or negative is put together to give a general impression. To do this three algebraic processes/models can be used:

- **Summation**: an impression is created by adding together each piece of information about an individual.
- **Averaging**: there is an averaging of the characteristics of a person such that they are seen as more favourable if, on the whole, they display more positive attributes.
- **Weighted average**: an impression is created by giving weight/value to pieces of information about the person, and this links back to the idea of Asch's (1946) central traits where some characteristics are seen as more important than others.

Tajfel and Turner's self-categorisation and self-identity theory (1957, 1959)

Found that we use categories in forming stereotypes and get an accentuation principle. Categorising means perceiving the similarities and differences between groups, and these are perceived especially when the category is important or relevant to the individual. Knowledge of the self is also derived from group membership, which produces a sense of social identity. Group membership encourages behaviour to be attributed to the self and "ingroup". Social identity theory thus states that individuals need to maintain a positive sense of personal and social identity and this is partly achieved by emphasising the desirability of one's own group, focusing on distinctions between other "lesser" groups.

Handy Hints for Evaluating the Work of Key Thinkers

- Consider how a central trait can be defined or operationalised and what the difficulties of this might be. For example, is it simply a correlation between different factors or is based more on context?
- Cognitive algebra is a complicated process and only some aspects may be of importance to some people.
- The extent to which impressions are formed as a result of group membership rather than on an individual basis needs to be considered.

Categories, Prototypes and Schema Use and Development

Categories and prototypes are used, and the relationship between categories is hierarchical. We use/rely on prototypes and examples from life and associative networks so that ideas about people can be connected.

Schemas provide order and structure to a complex social world, but schema use/type may depend on: the difficulty of the judgement; the degree of certainty; the need to process information; and individual differences in the ability to access information.

Both schemas and scripts are used to form impressions of others. Different types are used, including people schemas (individual pieces of information about a person), role schemas (knowledge about roles), scripts, content-free schemas (limited rules for processing information) and self schemas (knowledge about the self).

Acquisition and development involves the following processes:

- becoming more related to experiences as these broaden;
- becoming more complex with experience;
- becoming better organised and compact as a factor of complexity; and
- becoming more resilient to expectations and more accessible.

Rothbart (1981) in Hogg & Vaughan (2005) state that there are three processes involved in schema change, including:

- **Bookkeeping**: a general change in light of new evidence.
- **Conversion**: after the presentation of inconsistent information there is a sudden change.
- **Subtyping**: schema change as a result of forming subcategories.

Social Encoding

The social world is processed by the individual and involves:

- **Preattentive analysis**: the unconscious taking in of information.
- **Focusing of attention**: considering the identification and categorising of information.
- **Comprehension**: give it a meaning.
- **Elaborative reasoning**: the linking together and elaboration of information.

Information may be better socially encoded when it is vivid (information that is emotionally interesting, provokes images and is environmentally close and therefore more salient) and also more accessible or easily recalled (primed).

Handy Hint for Evaluating Social Encoding

- Consider if research on social coding has become too cognitive based and no longer social, as cognitive decisions may not be affected by social context.

Person Memory

Focuses on a prepositional model of memory. The idea is that we store propositions and ideas that are linked by associations, with some of these being stronger than others. This is enhanced by rehearsal. Recall involves the use of these links and more is remembered when there is inconsistent information as this involves more thoughts/the use of more links.

Person memory is therefore made up of traits and is organised into a range of socially desirable and competent traits. Behaviour is organised according to goals and appearance is based on observation. Impression can then be organised according to the person or group.

> *Preference is usually to make inferences about the person, although there may be some preference for forming impressions using the group when we first encounter a stranger, as stereotypes are used in this instance.*

Social Inference

We use social assumptions to make judgements and form impressions of others. This can involve two processes: top-down, which generally relies on schemas and stereotypes; and bottom-up, which focuses on specific events and information.

Social inference is, however, prone to errors, which means that ideal processing for making accurate judgements are not in place. Such errors occur in:

- **Gathering and sampling** of information as there is a reliance on schemas (especially person schemas) which may mean that one ignores important information or exaggerates unimportant information.
- **Regression**, where initial judgements tend to be extreme but gradually regress to represent average feelings/experiences.
- **Making judgements**, where base rate information or factual/strategic information is underused, which leads to bias.
- **Covariation and illusory correlation**, where incorrect judgements about the relationship between two events may be made because they are usually associated (given associative meaning) or paired because of some unusual distinction (paired distinctiveness).

Tasks

1 Look up Asch's study (1946) where participants were presented with descriptions of hypothetical people and were then asked to describe their overall impression of that person, following variations of several

key/"central" traits. Outline this study and record how it shows support for the configuration model that Asch proposed (see Key Thinkers).

2 Using your textbook, identify studies which show that schemas and stereotypes do influence social cognition/the impressions we form of others.

3 For each of the studies identified in task 2, write a paragraph specifying how these research studies show a link between schemas/ stereotypes and social cognition, and then bullet point the problems of this possible link, or the problems of the research studies themselves.

" Discuss research into the nature of social representations. "

This question requires you to show your understanding of social cognition, what it is and the processes involved. Most critically, you will need to focus on the work of the key thinkers to show how each of them believe we create impressions of others. Since the essay specifically asks you to refer to "research", it will be necessary to outline the studies upon which each of these theories are formed and any problems of such theories.

" Critically evaluate psychological research into schemas and stereotypes. "

Since research into the use of schemas and stereotypes is fundamental to this topic, it will be necessary for you to outline the contribution they make to social cognition in an initial introduction. Tasks 2 and 3 above are then designed to aid your answer to this question as you then need to show how these principles actually apply in practice, showing evidence for these processes in research studies. Be specific about the evidence for them and do not then forget to consider any problems with their involvement in social cognition and any methodological difficulties in the studies.

Common Pitfalls

- Do not forget to evaluate.
- Do not assume the processes described are bad, for example, stereotyping, as they are actually useful in helping to make sense of the world.
- Ensure familiarity of terms and stages, for example, of schema use.
- Make sure you learn each of the theories with their supporting studies and do not assume that simply describing a theory will gain you marks.

Textbook guide

ASCH, S. E. (1946). Forming impressions of personality. *Journal of Abnormal and Social Psychology, 59*, 177–181. An in-depth look at the study and theory proposed by Asch.

ABRAMS, D. & HOGG, M. A. (1999). Social identity and social cognition. Oxford: Blackwell. Coverage of the topic from a wide range of authors. A more thorough look at cognitive algebra using the original paper.

ANDERSON, N. H. (1965). Adding versus averaging as a stimulus combination rule in impression formation. *Journal of Experimental Psychology, 70*, 394–400. More in-depth look at this original explanation for impression formation.

FISKE, S. T. & TAYLOR, S. E. (1991). Social cognition (2nd ed.). New York: McGraw-Hill. A mainstream text providing comprehensive coverage of this whole topic.

2.3

attribution

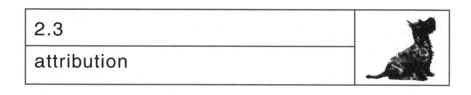

Core Areas

- Actor-observer effect
- Attribution
- Correspondent interference theory
- Covariation/ANOVA model

- Emotional lability
- Fundamental attribution errror
- Internal and external attribution
- Self-serving bias

Learning Outcomes

By the end of this chapter you should be able to:

- outline and evaluate the key theories of attribution; and
- understand the main errors that affect the attribution process.

Running Themes

- Compliance
- Internalisation
- Social influence

- Normative social influence
- Informational social influence
- Individual centred approach

Introduction

Attribution is 'the process of assigning causes of our own behaviour to that of others' (Hogg & Vaughan, 2005).

Attribution refers to the process of understanding and thinking about people within social situations, as one tends to try and explain the behaviour of others. When making attributions, decisions about the causes of behaviour may depend on a number of different factors including personal characteristics and the social situation.

Key Thinkers

Rotter's theory of internal and external attribution (1966)
Is based on a 29-item questionnaire measuring locus of control. Rotter believed attributions could be either internal, where one feels they have control of behaviour and is personal, or external, where things occur due to chance and are largely the result of the environment.

Heider's theory of naïve psychology (1946, 1958)
Found that people inevitably construct theories about themselves and the world, so are 'naïve psychologists'. We do this because we like to believe behaviour is motivated and is predictable/controllable. This involves making internal and external attributions, that is, distinguishing between personal and environmental factors.

Jones & Davis's correspondent inference theory (1965)
Deduces that people make attributions based on, or corresponding to, underlying traits, drawing on freely chosen behaviour, whether behaviour is common/expected or not, if it is socially desirable, has important

consequences or if it is personal or not. Put simply, this theory simply says that people try to explain behaviour by finding a match between the behaviour they can see and the stable qualities/personality traits of the person displaying it.

Kelley's covariation/ANOVA model (1950, 1967, 1972)

Illustrates that our knowledge of behaviour is used to make attributions based on the consensus, consistency and distinctiveness of the available information. It looks at how such information co-varies with each other so, is there consensus (do other people behave in the same way as the individual?), consistency (has the individual behaved in the same way in the past, or on each occasion?) or, is there distinctiveness (where different behaviour is shown in similar, but different, circumstances)? According to this model an internal (person) attribution will be made when there is low consensus and distinctiveness but high consistency, otherwise an external (situational) attribution is made. If consistency is low, causes are discounted and alternatives sought.

Weiner's attribution theory (1986)

Demonstrates that he was interested in the attributions made for experiences of success and failure and believed that these were made based on three areas: locus, which could be internal or external (see Rotter above); stability, which is whether the cause is stable or changes over time; and controllability.

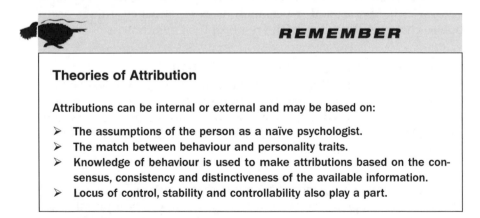

REMEMBER

Theories of Attribution

Attributions can be internal or external and may be based on:

➢ The assumptions of the person as a naïve psychologist.
➢ The match between behaviour and personality traits.
➢ Knowledge of behaviour is used to make attributions based on the consensus, consistency and distinctiveness of the available information.
➢ Locus of control, stability and controllability also play a part.

Schachter's theory of emotional lability (1964)

Shows that experience of emotion depends on attributions made about those feelings. They involve a physical component which leads to arousal, but also a cognitive component. This relies on the label given, or attribution made, and it is this attribution that will then determine the actual emotion experienced. When tested in a study by Schachter & Singer (1962) it was found that, when students were placed in a room with a stooge who behaved either euphorically or angrily, the emotion and behaviour experienced by this individual depended on the attribution they gave. For example, some students had been given an injection of adrenalin, some a placebo. They were then told the truth about the effect of the drug, misinformed or given no information. The misinformed group were more likely to behave in the same way as the stooge because they had little accurate information and so attributed their behaviour to situational factors. Those who knew otherwise simply made attributions based on facts and therefore experienced different emotions/displayed different behaviour.

Bem's theory of self-perception (1967, 1972)

Is where we derive a sense of self and identity by making attributions, so we examine our own behaviour which allows us to self-attribute/make assumptions about ourselves and our attitudes.

Handy Hints for Evaluating Theories of Attribution

- Correspondent inference theory is limited in a number of ways, for example, it looks at unexpected variations in behaviour when making social comparisons and therefore ignores past behaviour or stereotypes. It also fails to look at the importance of non-intentional behaviour.
- The covariation model poses problems, since we do not always have all of the facts on which to make judgements about a situation and therefore do not base judgements on consistency, distinctiveness and consensus. It is also possible that people respond to the most noticeable features of the situation.
- Similarly, Weiner's theory (1986) assumes that people make logical attributions using control and stability, but in reality there are many individual differences in the way that people see things. It is also possible that the three dimensions he discussed do not bear equal importance when making attributions.
- The difficulty with emotional lability is not only that the original study was methodologically flawed, but also that the role of cognitions in emotion is a problematic one since both emotion and attribution tend to be more spontaneous than this predicts.

> *Most of these theories can be criticised for the same reason, that is, attribution is less conscious than they all suggest.*

Attributional Bias

Research has shown that a number of errors/biases occur when making decisions about one's own or others' behaviour.

Fundamental attribution error

People tend to blame behaviour on the individual and their characteristics, and see the individual as responsible for their own actions. Thus internal, dispositional attributions are made. This occurs because one likes to feel that the world is controllable and therefore placing blame on stable personal characteristics is easier than considering changeable ones; attention also tends to focus on the immediate individual rather than other factors involved in the situation. Focus of emotion, theories of forgetting, cultural, developmental and linguistic factors could all account for this error.

Actor-observer effect

This can lead to error, as attributions about our own behaviour tend to be external and unstable, but for others it tends to be internal and stable. This may be because we do actually have different perspectives on behaviour and so perceive others' behaviour as more important and noticeable than our own.

False consensus effect

Since consensus was an important factor in Kelly's (1950) model, its role has been closely examined and it has been discovered that errors occur because we tend to assume that our behaviour is typical, even when this may not be the case, and therefore assume that everyone else would make the same assumptions. This is most likely to occur when we have strong beliefs about something.

Self-serving bias

Errors are made to ensure that our self-esteem is protected and therefore in order to 'serve ourselves' a bias operates whereby we take credit for our successes (so view them internally), but not for failure (so see failure as due to external factors). In part this maintains a sense of control and also a belief in a just world.

Attributional bias occurs as a normal social process and helps us adapt to the world in which we live.

Tasks

1 Using Table 1, fill in a description of each of the theories of attribution and an evaluation of each one.

"Evaluate" simply means considering the strengths and weaknesses of each theory using research studies and evidence.

2 A football manager summarises his team's performance after the match and believes that failure to win was due to the strong competition of the opponents. The weather conditions and the fact that it was an away match also failed to aid his side, according to his beliefs. What sources of attributional bias would be operating in the explanations he has used? Explain your answer.

" Evaluate the contributions that theories of attribution have made to psychology. "

The focus of this question is the evaluation, and although this requires some outline of the theories it predominantly asks you to focus on the research evidence that supports the theory and the possible difficulties that each theory raises. Due to time constraints you will need to focus on a few key theories, but do not try to cover each one as this will simply result in too much descriptive material and will not allow you the time you need to expand on the strengths and weaknesses of the theories.

"To what extent is the process of attribution reliable?"

This question requires you to focus on the sources of attributional bias and to argue that although these are normal social processes, they reflect the fact that attribution is in fact an unreliable process prone to errors.

Common Pitfalls

- Attribution can be a confusing topic because there is some overlap with the terminology used in each of the theories. You must therefore make sure that you understand the key terms before you proceed, for example, what is meant by internal and external attribution.
- Once key terms are established you must be sure that you do mix up the various theories of attribution and the contribution made by each.
- When discussing any of these theories, you must ensure that you do not slip into giving purely descriptive detail but evaluate them using relevant research.
- If you have difficulty understanding the biases that operate it would help to think of situations relevant to you when they have operated.

Textbook guide

KELLEY, H. H. (1973). The process of causal attribution. *American Psychologist, 28,* 107–128. Looks at the original paper and explanation of causal attribution.

WEARY, G., STANLEY, M. A. & HARVEY, J. H. (1989). *Attribution.* New York: Springer-Verlag. Looks at applications of attribution in the real world.

WEINER, B. (1986). *An attributional theory of motivation and emotion.* New York: Springer. In-depth coverage of this theory.

Table 1   Theories of Attribution

	Description of model	*Evaluation of model*
Correspondence inference theory		
Covariance/ANOVA model		
Weiner's attribution theory		
Emotional lability		

2.4

attitudes and attitude change

Core Areas

- Aggregation principle
- Attitude
- Attitude formation
- Balance theory
- Cognitive consistency
- Cognitive dissonance
- Compatibility/correspondence theory
- Elaboration likelihood model
- Expectancy value models
- Expectancy value technique
- Guttman's Scalogram method
- Heuristics
- Heuristic systematic model
- Information integration theory
- Inter-attitudinal structure
- Intra-attitudinal structure
- Likert's summated ratings scale
- Mood-as-information hypothesis
- Semantic differential scale
- Persuasion
- Self-perception theory
- Theory of planned behaviour
- Theory of reasoned action
- Thurstone's equal appearing interval scale

Learning Outcomes

By the end of this chapter you should be able to:

- define the key terms and theories involved in this topic;
- understand that attitude structure may incorporate one, two or three components and that the cognitive consistency theories explain the relationship between these;
- outline the functions of attitudes;
- acknowledge that attitudes can be formed because of behavioural or cognitive explanations;
- examine the relationship between attitudes and behaviour;
- discuss (both describe and evaluate) theories of attitude change; and
- identify and evaluate the different ways in which attitudes can be measured.

Running Themes

- Compliance
- Identification
- Social influence
- Normative social influence

- Internalisation
- Majority social influence
- Minority influence
- Informational social influence
- Individual centred approach

Introduction

An attitude can be defined as 'a mental state of readiness, organised through experience, exerting a directive or dynamic influence upon the individual's response to all objects and situations with which it is related' (Allport, 1935: 150).

> *So it involves an attitude object/situation which is something a person has in mind, and involves a tendency to evaluate, based on experience, and is observable in cognition.*

Therefore the purpose of an attitude is to help people make sense of the world and decisions, and so they aim to guide our reactions and interpretations of events.

Attitude Structure

- **One component**: attitudes are simply made up of a feeling towards an object – a positive or negative evaluation of it.
- **Two components**: an attitude is a mental state of readiness and therefore guides some evaluation or response towards an object.
- **Three components**: attitudes include feelings (affective), behaviour (actions) and cognitions (thoughts).

> *The ABC of attitudes is made up of affect (feelings), behaviour (responses) and cognitions (thoughts).*
>
> *Attitudes are also permanent, linked to social situations and generalisable.*

Intra-attitudinal structure

Looks at the relationship between these single attitudinal components and how consistent they are. Fishbein (1996) believes that an attitude towards an object is simply the sum of "expectancy × value" = products, where only relevant features are attended to by the person. Within this there can also be attitudinal ambivalence, where favourable and unfavourable beliefs exist together.

Inter-attitudinal structure
Looks at the relationship between different attitudinal objects. Links to explanations such as balance theory (see later notes).

Cognitive Consistency Theories

Cognitive consistency theories emphasise the cognitive component of attitudes, since beliefs or schemas are the building blocks of an attitude. It is the idea that a person tries to ensure consistency amongst their cognitions.

Heider's balance theory (1946, 1958)
Focuses on three elements: a person (P); another person (O); and an attitude, object or topic (X). It is therefore a triad of three elements, and a person tries to ensure consistency, or a balance, between these because this is preferable. Altogether there are eight possible combinations of relationships between two people and an object – four balanced and four unbalanced. If there is not such cognitive consistency, then it motivates attitude change.

The sociocognitive model
Focuses on the idea of a single component and looks specifically at the evaluation given to an object believed to be represented by a label, evaluative summary and knowledge structure.

Attitude Function

Attitudes serve as conscious and unconscious motives and according to Katz (1960) have four functions:

1 **Knowledge function**: attitudes give us knowledge about events, objects and people that direct experience and simplify information.

2 **Utilitarian/adjustive function**: there is the expectation of behaving in a socially acceptable way, so such attitudes are displayed, at least publicly, to gain positive outcomes and avoid negative ones.

3 **Social identity/value expressive function**: our self-concept has some value in the expression of attitudes, it is part of our individual identity and values and establishes identity in groups.

4 **Ego defensive function**: this allows us to protect ourselves/our self-esteem.

Attitude Formation

Refers to how attitudes are formed from experience as they are thought to be the result of learning.

Behavioural Approaches

Direct experience
Most attitudes are the result of direct experience (positive or negative). This is related to Fishbein & Ajzen's expectancy value model (1974), since negative experiences will lead to the experiencing of negative attitudes. Mere exposure effect also accounts for attitudes, since exposure leads to an evaluation represented in an attitude.

Classical conditioning
Repeated associations can mean that a previously neutral stimulus is paired with a less neutral response and can therefore be powerful in the formation of an attitude.

Operant conditioning
Behaviour that results in positive consequences is likely to be reinforced and repeated compared to behaviour followed by negative consequences, and attitudes are therefore shaped by a system of rewards and punishments.

Observational learning
Attitudes are the result of modelling the actions or emotions displayed by real life or symbolic models, so attitudes are simply observed and imitated.

Cognitive Approaches

Information integration theory
Attitudes are constructed in response to information we have about objects. So, attitudes are formed by evaluating and averaging information that is collected, and stored, about a given object.

Self-perception theory
People form attitudes by analysing their own behaviour and making attributes about them.

Mood-as-information hypothesis
Individuals base their attitudes on evaluations they make about their mood, so use mood to provide information and evaluation of an object.

Heuristic processing
Decision rules are used to make a judgement/form an attitude, so use mental shortcuts/cues available from memory.

Persuasion
Attitudes can also be formed in response to persuasion.

REMEMBER

Attitude Formation

Attitudes can be formed because of experiences that have been simply learned, or alternatively as a result of information/thought processes.

Relationship Between Attitudes and Behaviour

Compatibility/correspondence theory
Attitudes predict behaviour if there is compatibility/correspondence in terms of the target, context, action and time. Behaviour can be predicted from specific as well as general attitudes.

Aggregation principle
Rather than looking at general measures of attitudes, those taken over time are better at predicting behaviour rather than specific examples as they reflect different situations and times.

Attitude strength
Strong attitudes influence behaviour more because they are processed more readily and are more easily accessible. Attitudes that are strongly linked to the situation are more automatic (automatic activation).

Other factors
Moderator variables including the situation and personality influence the relationship between attitudes and behaviour.

Expectancy value models
Predict that the course of action is determined by expected outcome and valence of this outcome with individual's choosing the course most likely to lead to positive outcomes. The *theory of reasoned action* (Fishbein & Ajzen, 1974; Ajzen & Fishbein, 1980) explained the link by stating that the key factor linking attitudes and behaviour is the predictability of behaviour by intention. This involves subjective norms (perception of others' beliefs), attitudes towards the behaviour, intention and actual behaviour. Behaviour will result if an attitude and social norms are favourable and perceived behaviour control is increased. The *theory of planned behaviour* then went on to emphasise the role of violation and suggested that predictable behaviour is easier if people believe they have control.

Handy Hints for Evaluating Expectancy Value Models

- Consider how behaviour control can actually be operationalised or measured.
- What about other factors, such as moral values?
- These theories assume that attitudes are rational and social behaviour intentional, reasoned and planned, which is not always the case.

Key Thinkers

Festinger's cognitive dissonance theory (1954, 1957, 1964)
States that if we hold beliefs, attitudes or cognitions that are different, then we experience dissonance – this is an inconsistency that causes

discomfort. We are motivated to reduce this either by changing one of our thoughts, beliefs or attitudes or by selectively attending to information which supports one of our beliefs and ignores the other (selective exposure hypothesis). Dissonance occurs when there are difficult choices or decisions or when people participate in behaviour that is contrary to their attitude. Dissonance is thus brought about by effort justification (when aiming to reach a modest goal), induced compliance (when people are forced to comply contrary to their attitude) and free choice (when weighing up decisions). Festinger & Carlsmith's study (1959) supported this. Students took part in a tedious experiment to which they then had to attract further participants, and were either paid $1 or $20 for doing so. It was found that students who were paid less reported more positive recall of their own participation as this created less dissonance. It has since been determined that the following conditions are needed to produce attitude change: a perception that the behaviour has negative consequences; personal responsibility for behaviour; and some physiological arousal.

Petty & Cacioppo's elaboration likelihood model (1986)

Shows that attitude change occurs as a result of persuasion, but that the effect this has depends on the degree of cognitive effort applied to the message. If it requires much effort a "central route" is used, which involves understanding the argument, picking up on the most important points and considering a balanced argument. When the message requires little effort, then a "peripheral route" is used. Personal involvement, accountability and negative mood all increase message elaboration, as do individual differences in the need for cognition (engagement and enjoyment in thinking about problems).

> Therefore elaboration determines the processes used and the likelihood of persuasion towards attitude change. This further depends on motivation and ability.

Chaiken's heuristic systematic model (1980)

A heuristic is a mental shortcut used in the processing of information. When a person has a personal involvement in a situation and attending is therefore important to them, then input/cognitive processes or analysis occurs (systematic processing). In contrast, when personal involvement is low, individuals instead rely on these mental shortcuts to decide on attitude change. Persuasive messages are often processed in this way as we have a sufficiency threshold where heuristics are used if they give us enough confidence in the attitude we wish to display. The "bias hypothesis" also predicts that when a message is mixed or ambiguous, then heuristics will be used initially, and this may then lead to biased systematic processing.

Handy Hints for Evaluating the Work of Key Thinkers

- In dissonance studies, social desirability bias operates as people want to appear to have consistent attitudes (even if this is not the case, as this avoids social anxiety). Thus the findings may not truly represent dissonance and attitude change.
- Although the elaboration likelihood model looks at a wide range of variables and their interrelationships, it is difficult to determine precisely when central versus peripheral processing will occur.
- The heuristic systematic model assumes that attitudes changed using such shortcuts will then be unstable and resistant to subsequent change, but research does not support this.

Attitude Change

Much of the work on attitude change is covered above when examining the key thinkers in this topic. Thus it occurs because of:

- **Dissonance**: attitudes change when there is an inconsistency in attitudes or beliefs held (see Festinger above).
- **Persuasion**: the characteristics of the person presenting the message, its content and the characteristics of the receiver influence the persuasibility and possibility of attitude change. According to Hovland, Janis and Kelley (1953), three general variables (the communication source, message and audience) are involved in persuasion and there are four steps in the process of attitude change: attention, comprehension, acceptance and retention. A source that has credibility and a message that is repeated induces feelings not just facts, focuses on mode of presentation and is trying to induce attitude change will inevitably be more persuasive (the message learning approach). Gender, self-esteem and individual differences amongst audience members also have an effect. The dual process models of persuasion detailed above (the elaboration likelihood model and heuristic systematic model) suggest that attitude change results from the mode of information processing used by an individual in relation to a message, this being dependent on processing motivation and ability.

REMEMBER

Attitude Change

Attitudes may change because of:

> Inconsistency in beliefs (cognitive dissonance)
> Persuasion – due to elaboration or heuristics

Measuring Attitudes

Thurstone's equal appearing interval scale (1928)
One hundred statements assessing extreme negative to positive attitude towards an object are collated and then evaluated, by judges, on an equal interval, 11-point scale until there are 22 statements (11 positive, 11 negative). The average position of each statement is then taken and the statements given to participants who select those with which they agree. Their attitude is then measured by taking an average score of these responses.

Likert scale (1932)
Attitudes are indicated by selecting a response ranging from strongly agree (5), agree (4), unsure (3), disagree (2), strongly disagree (1), usually designed such that the statements are divided between representing a positive or negative attitude. This helps control for the acquiescence response set (the tendency blindly to agree, or disagree, consistently with the statements).

Semantic differential scale, Osgood, Suci & Tannenbaum (1957)
This method asks respondents to indicate their response from a list of opposite word pairs (good/bad), and this semantic differential (the difference between meaning) is then used to assess attitude.

Sociometry, Moreno (1953)
Interpersonal attitudes are assessed whereby group members indicate a preferred partner for an activity and this is used to chart these interrelationships.

Guttman's scalogram method (1944)

Attitudes are measured by the degree of acceptability of various statements, with a single trait being measured along this continuum of acceptability. It is designed such that agreement with strong items correlates with agreement of weaker ones, and likewise for statements to which a person disagrees. Analysis then reveals an underlying attitude.

Handy Hints for Evaluating the Measurement of Attitudes

- These scales do not account for the physiological measurement of attitudes or actual overt behaviour; these are also useful measures.
- Using such scales present problems such as social desirability bias (giving the answers they believe are expected) and demand characteristics (giving the answer they believe is being demanded of them).
- Operationalising (defining) attitudes is in itself problematic, and the lack of common measurement makes it difficult to make comparisons of data.
- Those that use rating scales may lead to forced choice responses which do not actually reveal the individual's true response, but simply the best choice offered.

Tasks

1 Write down a summary of your attitude towards sex before marriage. Then identify how many components your attitude has, what functions can be identified and how your attitude on this topic has been formed.

2 Use your textbooks to research a supporting piece of evidence for each of the explanations offered for attitude change (dissonance, the elaboration likelihood model and heuristic systematic model). Specifically record how each one offers support for the explanation given.

3 Using your knowledge of measurement, use two scales to design a questionnaire assessing the relationship between attitudes to under-age drinking and behaviour in this area. Write up a summary of your findings and identify any problems you encountered when using your chosen scales.

" Critically discuss psychologists' attempts to change people's attitudes and/or behaviour."

Here you need to select theories of attitude change (dissonance andpersuasion – the ELM and heuristic processing). In order to assess whether psychologists can use these to produce attitude change, you need to outline each theory and then more critically discuss its usefulness. This requires you to produce a discussion on the psychological/research evidence that supports the idea that each explanation is successful – using perhaps one or two studies – and then discuss any problems with the explanations. This material should be frequently referred back to the question such that you weigh up psychologists' attempts.

" To what extent is the psychological measurement of attitudes useful and valid?"

This is an area that allows you to show not only your knowledge of social psychology, but also your understanding of its research methods. You may wish to select just a few of the attitude scales that can be used, or widen your essay to include all of those outlined above. Marks will be given not only for your description of each one, where you may like to give written examples of sample statements, but also for the strengths and weaknesses of each, and the notion of attitudinal measurement generally. You could give examples of where the scales have been helpfully applied in psychological research and the problems encountered. Do not forget that each time you write down a piece of evidence, it should be referred back to the question so that you say whether or not this shows the scales to be useful/valid.

Common Pitfalls

- Attitudes and attitude change are big areas and you need to be clear on the content and terms involved. There will be an overlap; for example, attitudes can be formed because of dissonance and also changed due to this, but do not allow this to cause confusion. The breakdown above should help simplify the explanations given.
- As with all topics, do not just take the explanations offered at face value but instead take a critical approach – show an understanding of the psychological evidence to support the theories and the notes of caution that can be applied. Both the handy hints and tasks above will guide you on this.
- When studying attitude formation be clear about which explanations are behavioural (based on the learning of attitudes) and which are cognitive (look at information processing or thoughts).
- Remember that no one way of measuring attitudes is the correct way. It will depend on both the hypothesis being tested and the participants involved.

Textbook guide

AJZEN, I. (1988). *Attitudes, personality and behaviour.* Milton Keynes: Open University Press. This examines the whole field in more detail and is specifically devoted to attitudes.

EAGLY, A. H. & CHAIKEN, S. (1993). *The psychology of attitudes.* San Diego, CA: Harcourt Brace Jovanovich. Written by one of the proposers of the heuristic systematic, this gives a good review of theory and research into this area.

FESTINGER, I. (1957). *A theory of cognitive dissonance.* Stanford, CA: Stanford University Press. Original coverage of this theory.

PETTY, R. E. & CACIOPPO, J. T. (1986). *Communication and persuasion: Central and peripheral routes to attitude change.* New York: Springer. Particularly useful if you want to know more about how persuasion changes attitudes.

2.5	
social influence	

Core Areas

- Compliance
- Conformity/majority social influence
- Informational social influence
- Minority social influence

- Normative social influence
- Obedience
- Social influence

Learning Outcomes

By the end of this chapter you should be able to:

- define key terms;
- acknowledge the work of key thinkers in this area and be able to evaluate the work of the key thinkers; and
- show an awareness of the reasons for conformity, obedience and minority social influence.

Running Themes

- Compliance
- Identification
- Internalisation
- Majority social influence
- Minority influence
- Social influence
- Normative social influence

- Informational social influence
- Collective mind
- Individual centred approach
- Socio-centred approach
- Social norms
- Deindividuation

Introduction

Social influence is where people are influenced by others such that they try to display the attitude or behaviour of the social group either by obeying or conforming to the majority or the minority. Social influence occurs because of normative and informational social influence.

> *To help you remember what each type of influence means, normative (normal) is the desire to be* liked *and informational (information) means the desire to be* right.

There are different types of social influence, most of which focus on the majority view, for example, conformity or obedience. This is where people either change their behaviour so that they adopt that of the majority (conformity), or where they behave as they are told to, usually by a figure they perceive to have some authority over them.

Sometimes, however, the minority may be influential and this tends to occur when a minority presents a consistent argument that may then influence the attitudes and behaviour of the majority.

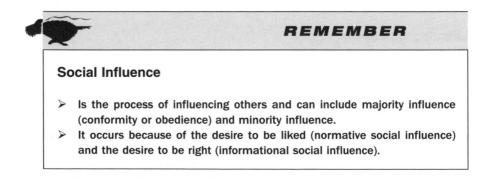

REMEMBER

Social Influence

➤ Is the process of influencing others and can include majority influence (conformity or obedience) and minority influence.
➤ It occurs because of the desire to be liked (normative social influence) and the desire to be right (informational social influence).

Some psychologists do not believe that there is such a distinction between these two processes, however, and instead propose a dual process model of dependency where they claim that they operate together, simply because we are dependent on others for information as well as social acceptance. It is therefore possible that these processes are not as distinct as was at first thought.

Key Thinkers/Research

Sherif's autokinetic effect (1935a)

Experiment asked people to judge how far a (stationary) light had moved when it was projected onto the wall of a darkened room (this is the auto-kinetic effect, as the light can appear to move in these circumstances). They were tested individually and then in small groups, and it was found that their individual judgements gradually began to conform to a group norm – that is, a generally agreed answer despite the fact that the light had not actually moved. Thus, people were subject to majority social influence/conformity.

Asch's line experiment (1956)

Aimed to see if people would conform to an obviously incorrect answer given by others in a group, concerning the length of a line. Students were asked to judge whether or not a standard line matched a compari-son one, and were also seated near the end of the group such that all of the previous participants/stooges gave the incorrect answer first. There was a mean conformity rate of 32 per cent, but this varied when vari-ables affecting conformity were changed. For example, the size of the majority, losing or gaining a partner, task difficulty/nature of the task and mode of response reduced conformity. It appears that people conformed either because there was a genuine distortion of perception or due to normative social influence.

Haney, Banks & Zimbardo's prison study (1973a)

Required that volunteers took part in a simulation where they were randomly assigned the role of a prisoner or guard and taken to a converted university basement resembling a prison environment. There was some basic loss of rights for the prisoners, who were unexpectedly arrested and given a uniform and an identification number (they were therefore dein-dividuated). The study showed that conformity to social roles occurred as part of the social interaction, as both groups displayed more negative emotions and hostility, and dehumanisation became apparent. Prisoners became passive, whilst the guards assumed an active, brutal and dominant role. Although normative and informational social influence had a role to play here, deindividuation/the loss of a sense of identity seemed most likely to lead to conformity.

Milgram's shock experiment (1963)

Told participants that they were taking part in a study on learning where they were to act as the teacher. They were then responsible for going over paired associate learning tasks; when the learner (a stooge) got the answer wrong, they were told by Milgram that they had to deliver an electric shock. This did not actually happen, although the participant was unaware of this as they had themselves received a sample (real) shock at the start of the experiment. They were encouraged to increase the voltage given after each incorrect answer up to a maximum voltage, and it was found that all participants gave shocks up to 300v and 65 per cent reached the highest level of 450v. It seems that obedience is most likely to occur in an unfamiliar environment and in the presence of an authority figure, especially when covert pressure is put upon people to obey. It is also possible that it occurs because the participant felt that someone else, other than themselves, was responsible for their actions.

Moscovici, Lage & Naffranchoux's slide study (1969)

Asked participants to judge the colour of 36 slides, all blue, and asked to say aloud both the colour of the slide and to estimate the light intensity. They were allocated to either a consistent condition, where the minority/stooges incorrectly described the slides as green, or the inconsistent condition, where 24 slides were described as green and the remaining 12 correctly as blue. They were then asked the colour of the slides with the number of "green answers", indicating conformity to minority social influence. This occurred 8.42 per cent of the time in the consistent condition, compared to 1.25 per cent of the time in the inconsistent condition; thus minority influence can occur in these conditions.

Handy Hints for Evaluating the Work of Key Thinkers

- Many of the criticisms for these studies focus on the research methods used and the ethical issues. For example, many have claimed that social influence was simply demonstrated because of the experimental methods used and

that within the wider context such work would lack validity. Findings therefore simply lack ecological validity and experimental realism. Demand characteristics may have also played a role as it was not difficult for participants, in any of these studies, to guess the real aims and therefore act accordingly.
- The ethical issues involved in these studies can be considered as a whole topic in themselves, but some awareness of them is critical. For example, was consent really obtained in each of these studies and can the deception used be justified? Milgram himself argues that deception was actually necessary within this context and that those interviewed after his study felt it was justifiable, although others believe that the studies simply infringed the rights of individuals to an unnecessary degree.

Reasons for Conformity

The processes involved in social influence are not inherently bad, as it is necessary to conform to social roles to operate within society. As these studies highlight, there are a number of reasons why conformity occurs.

- *Informational social influence*: people will yield to the majority social influence because they want to be accepted and therefore feel the need to be right/ display the correct answer or behaviour in order to gain such acceptance.
- *Normative social influence*: people have the desire to be liked by the social group and therefore conform to the behaviour and attitudes displayed by the majority.
- *Sociological factors*: both historically, culturally and sociologically, conformity has been encouraged and the costs of not conforming may be great. Children are encouraged to conform from a young age, and thus it is part of the socialisation process.
- **Group size**: in Asch's conformity study, it was found to be most likely the larger the majority.
- **Task difficulty**: when an individual is unsure (and a task difficult), then they are more likely to conform to the majority.
- **Individual differences**: people with low self-esteem, and females, are more likely than males to conform.

Reasons for Obedience

- **Environment**: obedience appears to occur in an unfamiliar environment.
- **Legitimate authority**: obedience occurs when people are in the presence of an authority figure whom they believe has some authority over them and when they want to be liked (normative social influence). If it is believed that when someone has expertise, we are more likely to obey their recommendations.

- **Agentic shift**: it is also the case that people obey because they feel that someone else is responsible for their actions (that is, the authority figure) rather than themselves.
- **Socialisation**: children are socialised from a young age to obey and learn that the costs of not obeying may be high. This is a sociological phenomenon, as in society non-obedience is a punishable offence.
- **Passivity**: some people prefer to avoid confrontation and therefore obey.

Reasons for Minority Social Influences

Minority social influence is most likely to occur when the minority presents a:

- **consistent** but flexible argument;
- when they are **committed** to their cause, against the majority's belief; and
- when there is **relevance** of their argument to current social thinking.

Tasks

1 There are several studies on the role of social influence including Sherif, Asch, Zimbardo, Milgram and Moscovici. Construct a table like that shown below and detail what types of social influence you believe are displayed in each of these studies and why you believe this to be the case. This will help check both your understanding of the studies themselves and the types of social influence.

	Types of social influence shown in this study	*Evidence to support existence of each type of social influence*
Sherif		
Asch		
Zimbardo		
Milgram		
Hofling		

2 List three situations in which you have previously conformed, and three in which you have obeyed. For each of these write a paragraph explaining your own behaviour, using your knowledge of social influence.

3 Write a list of criticisms for each of the studies you have covered. Underneath each of these expand and say exactly why each one criticises the research on social influence. You can use the Handy Hints provided above to help you do this.

"Discuss the view that studies of conformity and obedience demonstrate the process of social influence."

In your answer you need to show how normative, information or dual processes of social influence operate within research. This will require you to demonstrate a knowledge of the studies involved and also the types of influence, showing the examiner *where and how* the work reflects social processes.

"To what extent do studies of social influence resemble this process within the real world?"

In contrast to the question above, the emphasis here is on the evaluation of the studies. Your focus should not be on systematically describing each study but to take a critical approach to the work, providing evidence for the fact that although they undoubtedly demonstrate social influence this may in fact only be confined to the experimental context. You therefore need to engage in an active discussion about the application of these influences outside of the experimental situation.

Common Pitfalls

- Each study is quite distinct in terms of the methods it uses, but there is common ground in terms of the types of influence demonstrated and the application of each one to the wider context. It is therefore important that you are clear about the types of influence demonstrated in each study and that you do not mix up the studies. Task 1 above will aid clarification on this.
- Remember that the evaluation of these studies is mainly focused on their research methods and therefore you will need to understand the key terms involved, such as "ecological validity" and "mundane realism".
- There is a lot of material in this topic and you will probably not be able to cover every study, therefore you will need to be selective. Do not allow yourself to become entrenched in describing each piece of research as you will not have enough time left to evaluate it, so practice writing a precise synopsis of each one.

Textbook guide

ASCH, S. E. (1956). Studies of independence and conformity: A minority of one against a unanimous majority. *Psychological Monographs, 70* (9, whole No. 416). Original account of research studies.

MILGRAM, S. (1963). Behavioural study of obedience. *Journal of Abnormal and Social Psychology, 67*, 371–378. Original account of research studies.

MILGRAM, S. (1974). Obedience to authority. New York: Harper & Row. Includes coverage of all his major work in this field.

MOSCOVICI, S., LAGE, E. & NAFFRENCHOUX, M. (1969). Influence of a consistent minority on the responses of a majority in a colour perception task. *Sociometry, 32*, 365–380. An original account of the study.

2.6

group processes

Core Areas

- Distraction conflict
- Drive theory of social facilitation
- Evaluation apprehension
- Group socialisation
- Group structure
- Ringelmann effect
- Social cohesion/interpersonal interdependence model

- Social comparison theory
- Social facilitation
- Social impact
- Social loafing
- Task taxonomy
- Theory of group cohesiveness

Learning Outcomes

By the end of this chapter you should be able to:

- define key terms;
- acknowledge the work of key thinkers in this area;

- understand the effect on performance of group size including explanations such as social loafing, social impact and social comparison;
- examine theories on group cohesiveness;
- look at the process of socialisation within groups; and
- understand something of group structure, especially the contribution of roles, status and communication networks.

Running Themes

- Compliance
- Identification
- Internalisation
- Majority social influence
- Social influence
- Normative social influence

- Informational social influence
- Collective mind
- Socio-centred approach
- Social norms
- Deindividuation

Introduction

A group can be defined as "Two or more people who share a common definition and evaluation of themselves and behave in accordance with such a definition." Hogg & Vaughan (2005: 650)

To help you understand this definition it is helpful to remember that, according to Johnson & Johnson (1987), a social group is a collection of individuals who:

- *interact*
- *see themselves as a group*
- *are interdependent and interact with each other*
- *are trying to achieve a shared goal*
- *follow a common set of norms/roles.*

Key Thinkers

Allport's social facilitation theory (1920)
Examined whether the presence of others (the social group) can facilitate certain behaviour. It was found that an audience would improve an actor's performance in well learned/easy tasks, but lead to a decrease in performance on newly learned/difficult tasks due to social inhibition.

Zajonc's drive theory of social facilitation (1968)

Looked at how arousal "drives" social behaviour and increased arousal occurs as a natural instinct in the presence of others. As such increased arousal due to the audience may increase performance on well learned/ easy tasks, but impair performance when this is not the case.

Cottrell's evaluation apprehension theory (1972)

Found that it is not the presence of others that causes arousal, but the apprehension of being evaluated by others. If we are confident of our ability, then being watched/having an audience will increase performance, but if we are not confident and we are worrying about being evaluated, then our arousal increases because of evaluation apprehension and so performance declines.

Baron's theory of distraction conflict (1986)

Determines that we can only attend to a limited amount of information and therefore if performing a simple task we can also attend to the demands of the group, but if we try to focus on both types of demands then arousal increases and performance declines.

Steiner's task taxonomy theory (1972)

Deduces that in deciding whether a group performs better than an individual, there is a need to classify the task according to whether it is:

- divisible or unitary (whether there can be a division of labour or not);
- maximising (need to do as much as possible) or optimising (meeting a predetermined target); or
- an additive task (group output is the sum of individual input), a disjunctive task (group output is the result of one individual's input) or conjunctive (where output is determined by the input/performance of the slowest or least able member).

Tasks can therefore be classified **but** actual performance will always be less than potential due to process loss (potential is lost in the process of group members performing as individuals due to any of the above factors) and may also include co-ordination loss where the behaviour of members is not co-ordinated. So,

Actual productivity = potential productivity − losses due to faulty group processes

Ringelmann's Ringelmann effect (1913)
Looked at how individual effort on a task decreases as group size increases due to co-ordination and motivation loss.

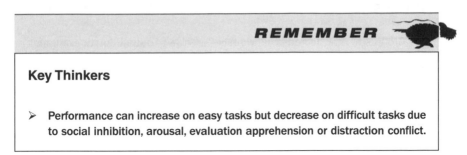

REMEMBER

Key Thinkers

➢ Performance can increase on easy tasks but decrease on difficult tasks due to social inhibition, arousal, evaluation apprehension or distraction conflict.

Effects of Group Size

Social loafing
Is where individual effort decreases (therefore one loafs!) when working in a group rather than alone, or with another. This is related to the free rider effect, where the member takes advantage of the benefits of being part of a group and exploits this without making any meaningful contribution.

Reasons for social loafing, according to Geen (1991), include:

- **Output equity**: The individual believes that efforts are decreased in groups and that others in the group also believe this, therefore to maintain equal output they also engage in such behaviour.
- **Evaluation apprehension**: Although there is more anxiety about being evaluated as an individual, within a group people believe that they are more anonymous and thus feel that they do not have to make much effort if unmotivated.
- **Matching to standard**: In the absence of a clearly defined goal, or standard to match, people tend to apply less effort.

Social impact
Means that the fact that we are part of a social group impacts on our behaviour and attitudes. Group size is especially influential, with our sense of responsibility more diffused the greater the group size.

Social compensation
Is when we believe that others will decrease their efforts in a group and so we compensate for this by working harder. It is therefore possible that groups work collectively harder than the sum of its individuals.

REMEMBER

Group Size

➢ Group size may decrease individual effort due to output equity, evaluation apprehension, matching to standard and social impact.
➢ It is also possible, however, that group size increases effort to compensate for this effect.

Group Cohesiveness

Group cohesiveness is the factor that binds the group together, giving individuals a sense of membership and group identity.

This will therefore vary between groups, contexts and times.

Festinger et al. theory of group cohesiveness (1950)

Proposes that attraction to a group and its members, along with the social interaction and interdependence provided by trying to achieve goals, leads an individual to feel a sense of cohesion towards a group. This feeling of cohesiveness then encourages continuity of membership towards that group and the following of the required norms.

Hogg's social cohesion/interpersonal interdependence model (1993)

Illustrates that cohesiveness occurs because individuals cannot achieve a goal alone so get together with others such that there is already some interdependence and co-operative interaction. This leads them all to feel goal satisfaction and a mutual sense of reward with interpersonal attraction.

In affirming this theory, Hogg states that a distinction must be made between personal attraction, which is an attraction due to preferences and a close relationship, and social attraction, which does not focus on individual factors but on common group membership.

Handy Hints for Evaluating the Social Cohesion Model

- The social cohesion model looks at the wider definitions of attraction and can therefore be equally applied to both small and large groups.
- Research evidence has supported this notion, for example, when individuals were placed with others that they should have liked, or disliked, interpersonal liking did not automatically lead to cohesion. This supports the idea that social attraction must, instead, be more important.

Group Socialisation

Group socialisation involves stages that initiate individuals into the group, through a process of commitment and adjustment to changing roles.

Tuckman (1965)
States that there are five stages that small groups go through:

1 **Forming**: members start to get to know each other.

2 **Storming**: members start to work through areas of disagreement.

3 **Norming**: a common sense of identity and purpose starts to emerge.

4 **Performing**: the group starts to perform and has shared norms and goals.

5 **Adjourning**: the group disperses as it has achieved what it aimed to or there is a loss of interest and motivation.

Moreland & Levine (1982, 1984)
Look at integration from a lifespan perspective. This involves:

- **Investigation**: group recruits members, formally or informally, and entry into the group is marked by role transition.
- **Socialisation**: the group shows the individual the norms of the group and the individual accommodates these and is accepted once they display such socialisation.

- **Maintenance**: there is negotiation of roles and there may be transitions (divergence) if anyone feels dissatisfaction. These can also be ritualised in "rites of passage", which are symbolic, serve as an apprenticeship and involve loyalty elicitation.
- **Resocialisation**: this may then be required before full membership is again attained.
- **Remembrance**: this occurs once membership is no longer in place.

Handy Hints for Evaluating Work into Group Socialisation

- This research is useful as it looks at the reciprocal nature of individuals within a group, that is, how individuals change to fit into the group and how they might then initiate group change.
- It also shows that three basic processes underpin group socialisation: a comparison of rewards of the group compared to alternative options; the reciprocal nature of commitment to the group; and the nature and normality of role transitions.

Group Structure

Roles
Like norms, are patterns of behaviour but between those within the group. They exist for the benefit of the group and can be formal or informal. People can also be assigned task or socio-emotional orientated roles. Roles emerge to ensure that there is a division of labour, set goals and advice on relationships between members, and to give them a place within the group.

Status
Is a commonly agreed view that is held concerning the value that certain roles, occupants of that role, or indeed whole groups may have. Higher status roles tend to be viewed commonly as valuable and are ones that encourage initiation of ideas that are then adopted by the whole group. Status hierarchies do, however, vary between contexts and times, although some are institutionalised. Status can derive from "specific status characteristics" that relate directly to the ability to perform the group task, and "diffuse status characteristics" that are more focused on the values they hold within society.

Communication networks

Are networks that provide rules on communications between different roles in the group. Models involve those including three, four or five members with greater performance being achieved on simple tasks when there is more centralisation, but this is less crucial on complex tasks because the complexity of information would overwhelm a single person. To be effective, both a formal and informal communication structure exists in most groups.

Tasks

1 Consider the following case study:

John is making his debut as a County Cricket player and his parents have come to watch his first match. He is very nervous as inevitably both his family and his team mates are hoping he will do well. Unfortunately he fails to take a wicket (get anyone out when bowling) and misses his opportunity to take a catch. He scores only 5 runs.

Using the theories proposed by the key thinkers explain the reasons for John's performance.

2 Think of a situation when you recently joined a social group. Using the psychological research provided in this chapter, explain what factors encouraged you to feel part of that group and what role you held within it.

3 You have been employed by a large company to set up a new work-force. You will need to advise them how to form this group of people, how to encourage the individuals to feel part of the group and how to be a productive workforce. Using your psychological knowledge, compile an action plan of two A4 sides to address these issue and then present this to your group.

❝ Using psychological theory and evidence, discuss the impact of groups on performance. ❞

Consider how the social group may affect performance. Refer to the main theories and evidence proposed on group size and say why each theory suggests that there is a decrease or increase in performance when part of a group. You also need to consider critically the explanations offered. For example, are there any studies to support the theoretical claims? What are the negative points about each explanation offered?

" Discuss the key factors involved in establishing and maintaining a productive group. "

You will need to consider the key theories as well as the impact of group size, cohesiveness, socialisation and structure. You should focus on key areas and demonstrate which factors are the most important when establishing and maintaining a productive group. Furthermore, you will need to take a critical approach to this and examine the factors that can prevent the establishment and maintenance of productivity.

Common Pitfalls

- There is a lot of research into group processes and it can be difficult to categorise where each theory belongs and not mix up the various areas. It will help you to draw a spider diagram to ensure that you are clear on what theory explains which phenomena.
- Remember to use the hints and tips provided when considering group processes since the research is not foolproof and not all processes will apply to every individual within different types of groups.
- Most theories also have differing views and it is important that you acknowledge this, for example, the proposals concerning group cohesiveness and group socialisation. Not one view can be accepted, but as a psychologist you must show an awareness of the various viewpoints.

Textbook guide

BARON, S., KERR, N. L. & MILLER, N. (1992). *Group processes, group decisions, group action.* Buckingham: Open University Press. Major review of this topic.

BROWN, R. J. (2000). *Group Processes (2nd edition). An Introduction to Group Processes.* Oxford: Blackwell. Introduction to group processes.

LATANE, B., WILLIAMS, K. & HARKINS, S. (1979). Many hands make light work: The causes and consequences of social loafing. *Journal of Personality and Social Psychology, 37,* 822–832. This looks at the original concept of social loafing in more specific detail.

2.7

intergroup relations, prejudice and discrimination

Core Areas

- Ageism
- Authoritarian personality
- Belief congruence theory
- Contact hypothesis
- Dehumanisation
- Discrimination
- Dogmatism/closed-mindedness
- Frustration-aggression hypothesis
- Minimal group paradigm

- Prejudice
- Racism
- Relative deprivation
- Realistic conflict
- Self-fulfilling prophecy
- Sexism
- Social norms
- Stereotype threat
- Stigma

Learning Outcomes

By the end of this chapter you should be able to:

- define key terms;
- understand that there are different types of discrimination and know the theories offered for prejudice;
- acknowledge the role the environment plays in prejudice;
- recognise the effects of prejudice; and
- understand how the contact hypothesis encourages the reduction of prejudice.

Running Themes

- Compliance
- Identification
- Internalisation
- Majority social influence
- Social influence

- Normative social influence
- Informational social influence
- Collective mind
- Individual centred approach
- Socio-centred approach
- Social norms

Introduction

Prejudice literally means a prejudgement. Baron & Byrne (1991) define it as "an attitude (usually negative) toward the members of some group, based solely on their membership of that group…"

According to Allport (1954b), prejudice has three components:

- **Affective**: feeling (usually negative) about an object/person (for example, hostility).
- **Behavioural/cognitive**: intention to act in a particular way. Allport believed there were various stages that prejudical behaviour goes through: antilocution (hostile talk, for instance), avoidance, discrimination, physical attack, extermination.
- **Cognitive**: beliefs about an object or person.

Discrimination is, therefore, this behavioural display of prejudice.

---

*To remember these components you simply need to remember the **A B C of prejudice.***

Types of Prejudice and Discrimination

Sexism
This is prejudice and discrimination on the basis of a person's gender. Usually this focuses on discrimination against women. It is promoted by the existence of stereotypes and sex role behaviour where there is a shared image of a social group and appropriate sex role behaviours. This may have originated because structurally men held more powerful positions. In psychology, evidence of sexism is found in the very fact that the most eminent historical figures are men.

Additionally, there is a division of traditionally female fields (for example, "people fields" such as educational or clinical psychology) and male fields (academia or more "scientific" areas such as cognitive psychology). Paludi (1992) believes this may be because the "gatekeepers" in psychology are men and they determine the career paths of others. Sexism is also maintained by the presentation of females within the media (for example, ideal body sizes for women but not men), and the process of attribution.

Racism
This is prejudice and discrimination on the basis of ethnicity or race. It has accounted for many acts of widespread genocide and in social psychology racism has focused on anti-Black prejudice, largely within the United States. New racism suggests that negative attitudes and behaviours

express themselves more subtly than was previously the case but nonetheless exist as aversive, symbolic, modern, ambivalent or regressive racism. All of these still represent negative attitudes or behaviours towards a racial out-group. Detecting racism can therefore be difficult but can be found in the descriptions given of situations, of words used, in schemas or stereotypical associations.

Ageism

This is prejudice and discrimination on the basis of age. Generally the negativity will be expressed towards the older generation, who are perceived to make little contribution to society compared to the young.

REMEMBER

Types of Prejudice

> **Sexism**: this is prejudice and discrimination on the basis of a person's gender.
> **Racism**: this is prejudice and discrimination on the basis of ethnicity or race.
> **Ageism**: this is prejudice and discrimination on the basis of age.

Other forms of discrimination include:

- **Reluctance to help**: to maintain disadvantage individuals, organisations or societal structure may show a reluctance to help minority groups in order to benefit their cause.
- **Tokenism**: a small effort is made to give the impression that help is being offered to the minority group in order to avoid accusations of prejudice/discrimination.
- **Reverse discrimination**: discrimination which favours a minority group. This may have short-term benefits.

Key Thinkers/Explanations of Prejudice

Adorno, Frenkel-Brunswick, Levinson & Sanford's authoritarian personality theory (1950)

Further to their studies of anti-semitism, Adorno et al. began studying prejudicial attitudes amongst white, non-Jewish, middle-class students.

They used interviews focusing on political ideas and childhood experiences and projective tests and scales including the measurement of anti-semitism, ethnocentrism, political and economic conservatism and potential for fascism (F scale). They found that a certain type of personality – the authoritarian personality – did exist. It referred to an individual who tended to be hostile, rigid and inflexible, intolerant and someone who therefore upholds traditional values and respects authority that may have originated in childhood. According to Adorno et al., who based their beliefs on psychodynamic principles, unconscious hostilities from childhood are simply displaced onto minority groups and so their own antisocial views are projected onto minorities, thus serving an ego defensive function. Altemeyer, (1988) rejected the psychodynamic input towards authoritarianism and instead suggested that it was simply an attitude comprising of conventionalism, aggression and submission leading to right-wing authoritarianism.

Dollard, Doob, Miller, Mowrer & Sears's frustration aggression hypothesis/scapegoating (1939)

Proposed that frustration always leads to aggression and that aggression is always caused by frustration. When frustration cannot therefore be directly expressed, then it is displaced indirectly onto others (hence one finds a scapegoat!). In this way prejudice is cathartic as it allows the release of emotional energy.

Rokeach's dogmatism/closed-mindedness and belief congruence theories (1960)

Suggest that dogmatism or closed-mindedness accounts for prejudice because such individuals have a rigid and intolerant cognitive style that predisposes them to be prejudiced simply because it is a way of think-ing. There is a resistance to change when encountering contradictory beliefs and a need to retain the existing belief system. In his belief congruence theory, Rokeach then proposed that prejudice derives from dissimilar views amongst people (there is incongruence).

Tajfel's minimal group paradigm and social identity theory (1957, 1959)

Found that when divided into artificial (minimal) groups, prejudice results simply from the awareness that there is an "outgroup" (the other group). When boys were asked to allocate points to other (which might be converted to rewards) and were told that they were either part of their own group or the outgroup, then they displayed a strong ingroup preference. That is, they allocated more points on the set task to boys who they believed to be in the same group as themselves. This can be accounted for by Tajfel & Turner's social identity theory (1979), which states that individuals need to maintain a positive sense of personal and social identity, and this is partly achieved by emphasising the desirability of one's own group, focusing on distinctions between other "lesser" groups. As such, prejudice occurs directly as a result.

REMEMBER

Explanations of Prejudice

Prejudice can be a result of:

➤ an authoritarian personality that is hostile, rigid and inflexible, intolerant, and someone who therefore upholds traditional values and respects authority;

➤ frustration that cannot be directly expressed and is therefore displaced indirectly onto others who act as a scapegoat;

➤ dogmatism or closed-mindedness, where individuals have a rigid and intolerant cognitive style that predisposes them to be prejudiced simply because it is a way of thinking or where it is derived from dissimilar views amongst people; and

➤ social identity theory, where in order to achieve a positive sense of personal and social identity one emphasises the desirability of one's own group, focusing on distinctions between other "lesser" groups, which leads to prejudice.

Handy Hints for Evaluating the Work of Key Thinkers

• There are serious methodological difficulties when looking at the role of the authoritarian personality, for example, acquiescent response set may have caused problems, experimenter and confirmatory bias may be involved and the data is correlational (childhood experiences may not be linked to prejudice in later life). Furthermore, this explanation doesn't account for the differing rates of prejudice throughout history and in different cultures so personality cannot be the only factor responsible for prejudice.

- The frustration aggression hypothesis/scapegoating ignores the social context, which is of paramount importance when looking at prejudice. It is insufficient to see prejudice purely on an individual basis, and to do so is reductionist. The exact interaction between frustration and aggression is unclear and it is too simplistic to assume that frustration will always emerge as prejudice.
- Dogmatism/belief congruence theories still see prejudice on an individual basis, and if prejudice is based on society's structure the similarity of beliefs has little part to play.
- In Tajfel et al.'s work the groups were artificial, so studies lack ecological validity. Conflict between groups does not always result in prejudice. The studies also imply that prejudice is simply a natural occurrence because of the need to achieve a social identity, and again this can be criticised.

The Role of Environmental Factors in Prejudice and Discrimination

Social norms
Prejudice can simply be viewed as conformity to social norms.

Relative deprivation
Linked to Dollard et al.'s ideas on frustration-aggression (1939), this claims that relative deprivation accounts for prejudice. That is, people experience relative deprivation, either of a fraternalistic nature (comparison between groups) or an egoistic nature (comparison between individuals) and this leads to frustration/aggression and subsequent prejudice as people feel they are not getting what they are entitled to.

Realistic conflict (Sherif, Harvey, White, Hood & Sherif, 1961)
Prejudice arises from conflict between groups, especially in the presence of competition. Sherif's robber's cave experiment showed that groups of unknown boys went through three stages when placed in summer camp. First, group formation (they divided themselves into two distinct groups), then intergroup competition and finally conflict reduction. Most critically in terms of research on prejudice, it was found that when a tournament took place there was an apparent conflict of interests as both

groups aimed to win and since this was not possible hostility emerged. Thus prejudice and discrimination could result from such a conflict in the environment.

> *Most of the key thinkers see prejudice as a result of individual factors, whereas the role of norms, relative deprivation and realistic conflict examines the interaction of groups.*

Effects of Prejudice

Dehumanisation
People have their dignity taken away; they are seen only as a group member based on shared characteristics and not as individual human beings.

Stigma
Individuals are seen only in term of some negative characteristic (within the social context) that they are believed to posses. These may be visible, such as race, or "controllable," such as smoking.

Self-worth, self-esteem and wellbeing
Discrimination and prejudice may decrease a sense of self-worth, lower-self esteem and threaten psychological (and physical) wellbeing, for example, anxiety and depression.

Stereotype threat
We feel threatened by the fact that we think we will be treated stereo-typically and judged according to negative stereotypes, and as a result behave accordingly.

Self-fulfilling prophecy
Prejudicial expectations influence social interaction such that the behaviour of others may be changed so that it conforms so that set expectation. Thus the self fulfils the prophecy or expectation.

Reduction

Contact hypothesis

Allport (1954a) proposed that prejudice can be reduced when there is contact between groups, and this can include equal status contact and the pursuit of common (superordinate) goals. Segregation leads to ignorance and reinforcement of negative stereotyping, but prejudice can be reduced by ensuring contact between groups such that they come to realise that there is some equal status and that each group is made up of individuals. If conflicting groups are made to co-operate with each other to achieve a common goal, then this may also reduce prejudice.

Tasks

1 Consider the recent Stephen Lawrence inquiry. Use this real-life case to discuss the types of prejudice that might have been evident.

2 Write headings for each of the theories offered for prejudice. Include Adorno et al.'s authoritarian personality, Dollard et al.'s frustration-aggression hypothesis, Rokeach's notion of dogmatism/closed-mindedness and his belief congruence theory and Tajfel's minimal group paradigm and social identity theory. Using your textbooks, look up one study/piece of research for each of these to show *support* for the theory.

3 Using Worksheet 1, match up each theory to its appropriate description and criticisms. You could do this by using arrows.

❝ Discuss one or more theories of prejudice. ❞

When a question asks for one or more theories it does not imply that you need to write down everything you know, but instead suggests that you are selective. It makes sense to select those theories which offer a different slant to each other, for example, one that looks at personality factors and another that focuses on the self (authoritarianism versus social identity theory). You need to show knowledge of your theory first, psychological evidence/research studies that support the explanation and then any criticisms. For higher marks you need to engage with this material and expand on why the research supports or criticises the theory you are discussing.

"To what extent can prejudice and discrimination be explained by personality factors?"

This question requires you to show a balanced argument and can be divided such that you explain and discuss the supporting evidence for the link between personality and prejudice, and then raise the notion that there may be criticisms for this approach. Once you have explained what these are you can then discuss the alternative argument, showing that other factors (including environment) might be involved and the support for these, but again the idea that these are not fool proof.

Common Pitfalls

- Make sure that you understand the differing types of prejudice and the effects it can have on people, as it will not affect every person in the same way and can be harder to spot in some instances compared to others.
- To ensure that you can tackle the questions above, it would help to make sure you are clear on the role of personality versus the other factors that could explain prejudice.
- When discussing the theories, try to ensure a balanced argument for these factors and do not forget to include both the support and the criticisms for each one. Most critically, you need to make sure that you understand exactly why each one offers support or applies caution, otherwise you cannot tackle the essay to the desired standard.

Textbook guide

ADORNO, T. W., FRENKEL-BRUNSWICK, E., LEVINSON, D. J. & SANFORD, R. M. (1950). *The authoritarian personality.* New York: Harper. Coverage of the original work on this personality type.

ALLPORT, G. W. (1954). *The nature of prejudice.* Reading, MA: Addison-Wesley. A general introduction to prejudice and its origins.

BROWN, R. (1995). *Prejudice: its social psychology.* Oxford: Blackwell. Very good recent coverage of the issues involved.

ROKEACH, M. (1960). *The open and closed mind.* New York: Basic Books. An in-depth look at this original explanation.

Worksheet 1   Explanations of prejudice and their criticisms

Adorno et al.'s authoritarian personality:

implies that prejudice is simply a natural occurrence because of the need to achieve a social identity and again this can be criticised.

Tajfel's minimal group paradigm and social identity theory:

groups were artifical so studies lack ecological validity and conflict between groups does not always result in prejudice

frustration that cannot be directly expressed and is therefore displaced indirectly onto others who act as a scapegoat

individuals have a rigid and intolerant cognitive style that predisposes them to be prejudiced simply because it is a way of thinking or where it is derived from dissimilar views amongst people

is reductionist.

Rokeach's notion of dogmatism/closed-mindedness and his belief congruence theory:

methodological difficulties – acquiescent response set – always appears to show anti-semitism and ethnocentrism; experimenter and confirmatory bias may be involved and the data is correlational

in order to achieve a positive sense of personal and social identity, one emphasises the desirability of one's own group, focusing on distinctions between other "lesser" groups, which leads to prejudice

personality that is hostile, rigid and inflexible, intolerant, and someone who therefore upholds traditional values and respects authority

the exact interaction between frustration and aggression is unclear and it is too simplistic to assume that frustration will always emerge as prejudice

explanation doesn't account for the differing rates of prejudice throughout history and in different cultures so personality cannot be the only factor responsible for prejudice.

Dollard et al.'s frustration-aggression hypothesis:

ignores the social context

sees prejudice on an individual basis, and if prejudice is based on society's structure the similarity of beliefs has little part to play.

2.8

close relationships

Core Areas

- Affection
- Cognitive/balance theory
- Dissolution
- Equity theory
- Evolutionary social psychology
- Exposure and familiarity
- Filter model
- Interpersonal attraction
- Learning/reinforcement

- Physical attractiveness
- Privacy regulation theory (PRT)
- Proximity
- Reciprocal liking
- Self-disclosure
- Similarity
- Social affiliation model
- Social exchange theory
- Stimulus-value-role model

Learning Outcomes

By the end of this chapter you should be able to:

- define the key terms;
- outline models of affection (privacy regulation theory, social affiliation model) and the effects that lack of affiliation may have;
- understand the different types of love;
- outline the work of key thinkers in this area;
- describe and evaluate the influences on attraction formation;
- describe and evaluate theories of attraction; and
- understand the stages involved in maintaining and in the dissolution of relationships.

Running Themes

- Compliance
- Internalisation
- Social influence
- Normative social influence

- Informational social influence
- Individual centred approach
- Socio-centred approach

Introduction

Interpersonal attraction looks at relationships, their beginning, processes, maintenance and dissolution/breakdown. Affection is the basic need for the company of others (humans). Models include:

- *Privacy regulation theory (PRT)* **(Altman, 1975, 1993)**: people have different needs for company, which they regulate themselves according to their need for privacy. This can operate between dialectic and optimisation principles so can very between times or match desired and actual levels.
- *Social affiliation model*: people need to regulate their social contact to achieve a balance (like homeostasis).
- **Effects of lack of affiliation**: studies showing long-term, maternal and sensory deprivation reflect that we have a need for others because without them there is short-term and irreversible long-term effects. Different childhood attachment styles also result in experiences of later romantic love so affiliation provides a fundamental basis for long-term mental health.

The difference between liking and loving is that liking is a positive evaluation of another but loving involves attraction, caring and intimacy, emotions, cognition and behaviour (Rubin, 1973).

Types of Love

Berschield & Walster (1978) theorised that companion love is an affection for others close to us, but passionate love is romantic.

Sternberg (1988) proposed a triangular model where consummate love comprises intimacy, passion and commitment, but if there is only a combination of any two of these, then it will be either romantic or companionate. This is therefore a multidimensional model.

According to Hatfield & Walster's three-factor theory of love (1981), variables that underlie love include a culture that acknowledges the concept of love, a love object and emotional arousal.

> *Love therefore depends on past learning about love, and the presence of both a love object and arousal.*

Stage Theories/Key Thinkers

Kerckhoff & Davis's filter model (1962)
Identifies the probability of two people meeting as being determined by demographic variables/social circumstances. Thus our social group is filtered, and we are attracted to those with whom we share similarities.

Next, further filtering is based on the sharing of common basic values, and then the relationship between emotional needs. This filtering process thus determines the relationship stages.

Murstein's stimulus-value-role model (1976, 1986, 1987)

Illustrates that originally attraction is based on a stimulus stage (external attraction/factors), then on the similarity of values and finally a role stage based on the successful performance of relationship roles.

Lee (1984)

Believed there are five stages to premarital break-up:

1 Dissatisfaction is discovered.

2 It is then exposed.

3 There is some negotiation about it.

4 Attempts are made to resolve it.

5 The relationship is terminated.

Duck (1992)

Determined that there are four phases to dissolution

1 **Intra-psychic phase**: assessment of personal costs and rewards.

2 **Dyadic phase**: confrontation and negotiation.

3 **Social phase**: involves and uses social networks.

4 **Grave-dressing phase**: events are analysed and people are made aware as a "getting over it" activity.

Handy Hints for Evaluating Stage Theories

- Consider whether relationships really do go through a set of fixed stages.

Attraction

There are several factors that influence the formation of attraction.

Proximity
Physical or geographical closeness may determine the probability of attraction (the "field of availables" (Kerckhoff, 1974)). This is important as those who live near are more likely to share beliefs, social class and so on, and also incur familiarity, a further factor in the formation of relationships. Reciprocation must be genuine for this to be part of attraction.

Exposure and familiarity
According to Zajonc's "mere exposure effect" (1968) the more exposure and familiarity the higher the preference, and as proximity leads to exposure it may include familiarity. This also leads us to feel more comfortable, hence increasing the chances of attraction. Familiarity is rewarding as it leads to participation in joint activities, increases self-esteem, eases communication and leads to reciprocal liking.

Physical attractiveness
We are drawn to people who are physically and psychologically attractive. Stereotypes dictate that we believe that those who look physically attractive are also psychologically attractive/have attractive personalities. What is defined as attractive varies according to cultural norms, but there are some generally agreed principles and tends to be based on averages. Links have also found that attractive people are defined as feminine, youthful, slim, honest, successful, well adjusted, happier and more intelligent.

Similarity
Attraction occurs because of the similarity of looks, beliefs, attitudes and values. The matching hypothesis is related to similarity as it suggests that people are most likely to show romantic investment if they are matched in their ability to reward each other, including a basis of physical attraction and similarity. People may also become more similar over time.

Reciprocal liking
The reciprocity principle suggests that we like those who like us, and vice versa for those whom we dislike. We are therefore most attracted

to those who like us; however, there are individual differences in this and our need to feel secure/self-esteem needs. This is due to the reward–cost model, that is, we are attracted to those who reciprocate and reward us rather than involving ourselves in personal relationships where there may be personal costs. Alternatively the gain–loss theory (Aronson & Linder, 1965) may explain this, where we are actually attracted more to people who start off by disliking us, before changing their minds, as here we gain liking. In contrast, we dislike those whom initially like us and then change their minds (and hence we lose reciprocal liking).

Self-disclosure

Attraction depends on self-disclosure/sharing of intimate feelings with another person, and is therefore important in developing and maintaining relationships as we tend to disclose information to those we like and those who disclose information to us.

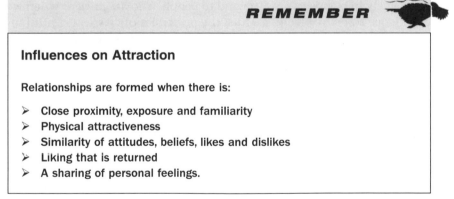

REMEMBER

Influences on Attraction

Relationships are formed when there is:

➢ Close proximity, exposure and familiarity
➢ Physical attractiveness
➢ Similarity of attitudes, beliefs, likes and dislikes
➢ Liking that is returned
➢ A sharing of personal feelings.

Handy Hints for Evaluating Influences on Attraction

- Although proximity is a factor, if people are too close it can reverse the effect as it makes us feel uncomfortable.
- Exposure and familiarity may work in the opposite way and lead to the discovery of negative characteristics.
- Remember, physical attractiveness is cultural, gender and context biased.
- Complementarity (Winch, 1958) may be more important than similarity, that is, the need to deliberately attract people who are dissimilar and who complement us so that our needs/resources are satisfied.

Theories of Attraction

Evolution

According to Darwin (1872), interpersonal attraction ensures evolutionary survival and has evolved as it therefore increases protection and reproduction.

Cognitive/balance theory

According to Heider's balance theory (1946, 1958), people are motivated to achieve a balance in relationships, or a sense of cognitive consistency whereby people are attracted to those with similarity and reciprocal attraction and beliefs. They will then make changes in a relationship if this is not the case, to restore the cognitive balance. Therefore a balance is sought between liking/disliking and positive/negative feelings/attraction.

Learning/reinforcement theories

Byrne & Clore's reinforcement-affect model (1970) shows that we are more likely to be positively attracted to people who are present when we experience a positive feeling. Thus, the principles of classical conditioning and operant conditioning apply, as attraction is seen as conditioned emotional responses and consequences of interpersonal behaviour/the reinforcement provided by the other person.

Economic theories

Relationships are simply a social exchange that depends on profits gained, thus still based on behaviourist principles. There is a cost–reward ratio involved; for example, a calculation of what costs are involved in receiving rewards from others. Social exchanges therefore form the basis of relationships for the benefits they provide relative to the input required as a joint process by both parties, with the aim of averaging mutual benefit/profits with minimal costs (minimax strategy). This will partly be judged by using a comparison level/standard for judging profitabilty. Attraction is most likely to occur if an exchange is seen to be a positive. The e*quity theory* views relationships as being based on a fair/equal balance of input/output, or rewards and costs, by both partners. Adams (1965) predicts that equity exists when A's outcomes divided by A's inputs equals B's outcomes divided by B's inputs. Such equity is guided by the equity norm, social welfare norm (resources are allocated according to need) and the egalitarian norm (everyone should get equal amounts).

> *If the ratios of input and output are felt to be equal, then a relationship will be established and maintained.*

If there is inequity, we alter our input or restructure our perceived input so it does not seem so unequal. If this does not work, then the relationship ends.

Handy Hints for Evaluating Theories of Attraction

- Evolution does have difficulty when explaining the complexity of human relationships, for example, cheating.
- Relationships are not just about averaging cognitive consistency between two people as they are influenced by the wider social context and we may be comfortable with others we know to be dissimilar.
- Some relationships exist in absence of rewards.

Maintaining Relationships

Commitment

The desire and intention to sustain the relationship. Increased commitment increases the chances of staying together and provides security. Commitment can also involve changing when need to, and making sacrifices. Johnson (1991) stated that people must want to consider the relationship, feel they ought to and must do so. Adams & Jones (1997) believed that personal dedication, moral commitment and constraint commitment are essential to the success of a relationship (otherwise it is costly to leave the relationship).

Role complexity

We need to complement each other's roles as this helps maintain relationships. We may also need to accommodate changes in circumstances and renegotiate roles. Roles can involve complementing needs and resources.

Similarity

As above, this helps maintain the relationship.

Dissolution

Dissolution is more likely to occur if one partner is younger than average, of a lower socio-economic group, of different demographic background or has experienced parental divorce as a child or married early. Other factors involved in breakdown include:

- **Physical environment**, including hardship and distance.
- **Boredom**, with a lack of stimulation.
- **Social environment**, including "field of availables" to which one can compare their relationship, and influence of family and friends.
- **Conflict**, especially breaking rules of trust and difficulties in compromising and resolving conflicts, especially if a distress maintaining pattern is used.

Levinger (1980, in Hogg & Vaughan, 2005) believed that there are four factors indicating the end of a relationship: a new life seems the only solution; attractive partners are available; there is an expectation that the relationship will fail; and there is a lack of commitment to continuing the relationship.

Tasks

1 Factors that influence attraction include proximity, exposure and familiarity, physical attraction, reciprocal liking and self-disclosure. You have been provided with some information and an evaluation of these, but no supporting studies. You therefore need to look up one study showing the role of these in relationship formation and be explicit about why it shows evidence for each one.

2 Complete Table 2, which asks you to describe and evaluate each theory of relationship.

3 Think of a relationship break up that you have experienced and record why this may have occurred/what stages you went through, using the psychological information you have studied.

" Critically consider research into interpersonal attraction. "

This asks you to include most of what you have studied in this chapter. You will need to define attraction and then use the factors that influence its formation and the theories to discuss the topic. Most importantly, the question asks you to "critically consider" – that does not mean simply copying out the chapter, but that you write down what you know, and then evaluate, the role of each of these. As it also asks you to focus on research, you will need to incorporate your research from tasks 1 and 2.

"Describe and evaluate research into the dissolution of relationships."

Here you can include a discussion on the theories and stages of dissolution, which will have been helped by your own analysis in task 3. Most crucially, your essay must include some reference to psychological studies which represent these stages and you need to specify how and where this is the case.

Common Pitfalls

- Remember to evaluate theories and not just describe them.
- The factors that are involved in the formation of attraction are important, but equally so is the psychological evidence for them and it is all too easy to focus on rewriting the list rather than discussing research on their application.
- Many students ignore the dissolution of relationships as a topic in its own right because there is less literature on it. Make sure you are able to cover this fully, as it can be set as its own essay.

Textbook guide

DUCK, S. (1992). *Human relationships (2nd ed.).* London: Sage. A look at the major works in the area of relationships.

KERCKHOFF, A. C. & DAVIS, K. E. (1962). Value consensus and need complementarity in mate selection. *American Sociological Review, 27,* 295–303. An original look at the basis of the filter model.

BYRNE, D. & CLORE, G. L. (1970). A reinforcement model of evaluative responses. *Personality: An International Journal, 1,* 103–128. More information on the role of learning and reinforcement in attraction to others.

Table 2 Theories of Relationships

	Describe theory	*Outline support for theory and say how it supports*	*Outline criticisms for theory and how they criticise*
Evolution			
Cognitive/ balance			
Learning/ reinforcement			
Social exchange			
Social equity			

2.9

aggression

Core Areas

- Catharsis
- Desensitisation
- Disinhibition
- Ethology
- Excitation-transfer theory
- Frustration-aggression hypothesis
- Instincts
- Role of norms
- Role of media
- Weapons effect

Learning Outcomes

By the end of this chapter you should be able to:

- define key terms;
- understand theories of aggression;
- acknowledge the work of key thinkers in this area;
- show an awareness of the personal situational factors that might effect aggression; and
- examine the role of the media on aggression.

Running Themes

- Individual centred approach
- Socio-centred approach
- Social influence
- Social norms
- Deindividuation

Introduction

Berkowitz (1993) sees aggression as an act "involving behaviour, either physical or symbolic, performed with the intention of harming someone."

The key to understanding this definition is acknowledging that aggression can be a physical or psychological act that is carried out with the specific purpose of causing harm, thus it is antisocial. Many different definitions have been offered and thus measuring aggression or operationalising it can be difficult.

Biological Explanations for Aggression

All biological explanations believe that aggression is an instinct, that is an innate drive which is goal directed, beneficial, adaptive and shared by the same species.

Psychodynamic

Aggression is an instinct whereby there is a conflict between the dual instincts of life and death, and therefore aggression is an instinct that builds up and must be released to reduce tension. Known as catharsis, aggression therefore aids the release of emotion. This may initially occur as self-destructive behaviour, which is then replaced as aggression towards others. It is seen as a desire to reach death or eliminate tension totally and return to a womb-like state.

Ethological

Behaviour is again seen as genetic, and this approach specifically focuses on evolution/the survival and functioning of a species. Aggression serves an important function as it establishes hierarchies and ensures "survival of the fittest" where it builds up over time and is released in response to certain environmental stimuli. Basically, aggression is therefore seen as adaptive.

Handy Hints for Evaluating Biological Explanations

- When evaluating these theories you may want to consider how much actual scientific evidence is available for them, or if such theories are even open to empirical testing.
- Freud's concepts of life and death instincts (Eros and Thanatos) (1920, 1923) are abstract concepts that cannot be seen and therefore explaining aggression on this basis presents problems.

- Since much of Lorenz's work (1966), and that of ethologists generally, relies on animal samples. How applicable it is to modern human behaviour is questionable. You may want to consider whether aggression is still only an instinct that ensures survival of the fittest.

Social Psychological Explanations for Aggression

Frustration-aggression hypothesis

Frustration always causes aggression and aggression is always the result of frustration. Aggression is therefore triggered by frustrating situations and events. Therefore people are driven to aggression in order to reduce frustration and thus to maintain a balanced internal state. Berkowitz (1993) modified this original hypothesis to suggest that frustration actually produces a state of *readiness* for aggression, but that cues in the situation are also important. This led to the idea of the "weapons effect", whereby aggression is produced more readily if a weapon is present (especially one associated with frustration) rather than a neutral object.

Excitation-transfer theory

Aggression is the result of learning, arousal or excitation from an external stimuli and an individual's interpretation of that arousal. Aggression is therefore a result of a sequence whereby arousal is generated and then labelled as a specific emotion which leads to such behaviour.

Social learning

Aggression is simply the result of reinforcement, observation and imitation where aggressive behaviour is therefore acquired through direct, or indirect, modelling. Previous experiences of aggression and the likelihood of it being rewarded or punished are key factors in determining whether or not it is displayed and maintained.

Social interactionalist theory of coercive action

Aggression is the result of trying to achieve social power to control others, restore justice or assert/protect identities. This may involve harm or injury.

Role of norms

According to the norm of reciprocity, aggression may simply result from the fact that someone who is the victim of aggression feels that it is the norm to reciprocate this and therefore behaves in a similar way. If such behaviour is the norm, it is also the case that behaviour is more likely to be labelled as aggressive.

Social information processing

Both the situation and cognitive processes explain aggression because norms and schemas (a building block of existing knowledge) mean that information about the situation is processed and decisions made. This typically involves perceiving cues in the situation, interpreting them, examining one's own goals and responses and behaving appropriately. If a cue appears and is interpreted as aggressive, this information will be processed and produce subsequent aggressive responses.

> *Theories of aggression represent part of the nature–nurture debate in psychology and can be placed neatly into biological explanations that believe it is due to nature and social/psychological explanations which believe aggression is due to nurture.*

REMEMBER

Explanations for Aggression

Aggression may be the result of:

➢ The struggle between life and death instincts
➢ The need to ensure survival of the fittest
➢ Frustration in the environment
➢ Arousal that is labelled and transferred across situations
➢ Learning, directly or indirectly, from models
➢ The result of trying to achieve social power
➢ Norms
➢ Processing and interpreting the situation as requiring an aggressive response

Key Thinkers/Research

Freud's psychodynamic theory (1920, 1923)

Believed that aggression was simply an instinct arising from the conflict between life and death.

Lorenz's ethology (1966)

Studies were based on animal instincts and that aggression ensures survival of the fittest.

Dollard et al.'s frustration aggression hypothesis (1939)

Argues that frustration causes aggression and that aggression is the result of frustration.

Zillman's excitation-transfer theory (1979)

Suggests that aggression is the result of learning, arousal or excitation from an external stimuli and an individual's interpretation of that arousal.

Bandura et al.'s bobo doll experiment and social learning theory (1963)

Found that children who had watched a model receive a reward for aggressive behaviour were then more likely to copy such behaviour. Three groups of children watched a video where an adult was aggressive towards a "bobo doll" and the adult was just seen to be doing this, was rewarded by another adult for their behaviour or was punished for it. Children who had seen the adult rewarded were then more likely to copy such behaviour.

Handy Hints for Evaluating the Work of Key Thinkers

- It can be difficult to operationalise/define frustration and it is not clear what types of frustration will lead to aggression, or indeed if it will produce the same response in all people. You therefore need to consider whether this explanation can be generalised.
- Excitation transfer theory is more useful because it does at least focus on the individual's interpretation of arousal, thus accounting for the individual differences between people.
- The ecological validity of Bandura et al.'s study is questionable as the same influences may not be true in a real-life situation.

Personal Factors

Gender/hormones

There appears to be some correlation between aggression and elevated testosterone, and males are socialised more early on to behave aggressively compared to females.

Provocation

Provocation can lead to aggression due to the reciprocity principle, where one responds to aggression with aggression.

Alcohol

Although the link is not clear-cut, there is some correlation between alcohol consumption and aggression.

Disinhibition

The norms that usually stop us from acting in a particular way are not present so this makes aggression legitimate.

Deindividuation

People lose their sense of individual responsibility and thus engage in antisocial behaviour. For example, research by Diener, Fraser, Bearman & Kelem (1976) found that when children wore trick-or-treat costumes that prevented them from being recognised, they were much more likely to engage in antisocial behaviour, stealing and so on.

Media and Aggression

According to social learning theory, violence portrayed in the media leads to antisocial behaviour in the real world as it simply enhances aggression.

According to Comstock & Paik (1991), media aggression will encourage aggression in the viewer under the following conditions: efficacy (if media aggression achieves one's goals or is unpunished), normativeness (if it is perceived as justifiable with no negative consequences), pertinence (if the viewer identifies with the role being played), susceptibility (if aggression is portrayed in conjunction with emotions).

Other areas of interest include desensitisation, cognitive interpretation and the role of erotica.

Desensitisation

Desensitisation explains media violence by claiming that exposure to violence decreases one's usual emotional responsiveness to it. One research study by Sheehan (1983), who studied 5–10-year-olds, identified a correlation between children's exposure to violent television and later real-life aggression, but only in the elder children. Consistency of aggressive tendencies, fantasy and parental characteristics also, however, played a role.

Cognitive interpretations

Images of violence lead to cognitions (schemas) which later develop into antisocial acts. This approach accounts for the *weapons effect* where there is an increase in violence following the presence of weapons. In a study by Berkowitz & LePage (1967) it was found that the number of electric shocks given to a confederate were greater when the student had themselves received shocks in the presence of nearby guns, thus precipitating violent schemas and increasing the incident of subsequent aggression.

Role of erotica

Although evidence is mixed and the design of many studies examining the correlation between erotica and aggression can be criticised, there are some general conclusions that can be drawn. First, it is apparent that the arousal felt as a result of viewing erotic material can increase the level of subsequent violence in men (towards women). Second, that exposure to violent pornography perpetuates a myth that women enjoy such violence and therefore the overall erotica desensitises men against aggressive behaviour and so maintain negative attitudes towards women.

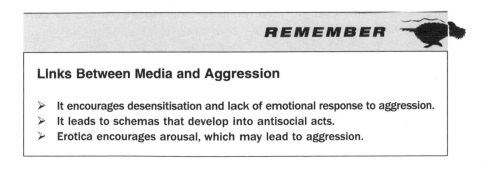

REMEMBER

Links Between Media and Aggression

➤ It encourages desensitisation and lack of emotional response to aggression.
➤ It leads to schemas that develop into antisocial acts.
➤ Erotica encourages arousal, which may lead to aggression.

Handy Hints for Evaluating the Relationship Between Media and Aggression

- Much of this work can be criticised on methodological grounds and there are particular points to bear in mind. For example, much of the data is purely correlational, meaning that it shows a *possible* relationship between the media, desensitisation, presence of weapons or erotica but a link between the two cannot be proven.
- It could also be argued that exposure to violence in the media simply alerts people to its effects rather than leading to desensitisation, and it is not the case that exposure to weapons or erotica always leads to aggression. It is therefore possible that many of the social, psychological and personal factors examined earlier act as mediating factors.

Tasks

1 Consider the following case study:

Laura, aged 8, has started to show aggressive behaviour at nursery school, which occurs mainly when she is trying to achieve something but has difficulty doing so, or if another child is playing with a toy that she wants. Her parents note that she had not shown such aggression until she started school.

Using the social psychological explanations of aggression, and the personal factors that might lead to aggressive behaviour, explain why Laura may be behaving in this way. Justify your argument and record any problems with your explanations.

2 There are a number of films portraying violence. Choose three that you are aware of and using evidence linking the media and violence (desensitisation, cognitive interpretations and the role of erotica) discuss how viewing each of these films (or any experience of your own) might lead to real-life violence.

3 Write a list of four reasons why evidence linking the media and violence are inconclusive. Using Table 3, record *why* each of these presents a problem.

Table 3   Reasons Why Evidence Linking the Media and Violence are Inconclusive

Evidence	*Reason why it is inconclusive*
1.	
2.	
3.	
4.	

66 Compare and contrast theories of aggression. 99

Begin by selecting the key theories, as it will not be possible to cover every explanation adequately. Preferably balance the argument by taking a selection from both the biological and the social/psychological explanations. This question requires more than a simple discussion of each theory; you should specifically compare (say what is similar) and contrast (say what is different) about them. By picking a range you can look at the differences in nature versus nurture, but you must ensure that you do this by referring back to the research evidence.

"To what extent does research show a relationship between the media and aggression?"

This question requires you to show both sides of the argument – the idea that there is some correlation between the media and aggression but that there are difficulties with this link. You may like to consider various types of media rather than television alone, which has been the main focus of psychological research, for example, the role of computer games. An outline of the role of desensitisation, cognitive interpretations and erotica can be supported by research studies that give the theories some credibility in proving a link. However, this must then be balanced by careful consideration of the problems of such work, the general issue of correlation and the idea that if the media is capable of producing antisocial behaviour, then it must also be capable of asserting some influence over prosocial behaviour.

Common Pitfalls

- Be sure that you do not mix up those explanations which focus on biology versus those that look at social psychological factors as they each have very different origins – one on the idea that it is due to nature and the other that it is due to nurture.
- When discussing the theories of aggression, ensure that they are supported by the relevant key studies, for example, that Dollard et al. supported the frustration-aggression hypothesis. It is not sufficient just to outline the theory, but you must ensure that you show yourself to be a true psychologist and back up what you say with actual evidence.
- It is a common mistake to assume that the media is responsible for aggression and when discussing this issue you must ensure that you give a balanced argument – outlining the reasons why this might be the case as well as why research can be questioned. It is also useful to contemplate differing forms of media, not just television, and also to discuss the view that the media may have positive as well as negative effects.
- Do not just outline research, but remember to evaluate it – say why it has been useful or what the pitfalls are.

Textbook guide

BARON, R. A. & RICHARDSON, D. R. (1994). *Human aggression*. New York: Plenum. Coverage of all aspects on the psychology of aggression.

BERKOWITZ, L. (1993). *Aggression: its causes, consequences, and control*. New York: McGraw-Hill. Coverage of the psychology of aggression but focusing on his own perspective.

BERKOWITZ, L. & LEPAGE, A. (1967). Weapons as aggression-eliciting stimuli. *Journal of Personality & Social Psychology, 7,* 202–207.

GUNTER, B. & MCALEER, J. (1997). *Children and television.* London: Routledge. Looks at the effects of television and considers both sides of the debate.

ZILLMAN, D. (1996). Cognition-excitation interdependencies in aggressive behaviour. *Aggressive Behaviour, 14,* 51–64.

http://www.medialit.org/Violence/indexviol.htm   Links to the discussion on media violence.

http://www.yorku.ca/dept/psych/classics/Bandura/bobo.htm   Covers Bandura's bobo doll study.

2.10	
prosocial behaviour	

Core Areas

- Altruism
- Bystander-calculus model
- Cognitive model of bystander intervention
- Diffusion of responsibility

- Empathy arousal hypothesis
- Evaluation apprehension
- Pluralistic ignorance

Learning Outcomes

By the end of this chapter you should be able to:

- define key terms;
- understand the reasons/explanations given for helping behaviour;
- show an awareness of the reasons for bystander behaviour; and
- describe and evaluate research studies relevant to this area.

Running Themes

- Compliance
- Majority social influence
- Collective mind
- Socio-centred approach
- Social norms
- Deindividuation

Introduction

Prosocial behaviour is seen by Wispe (1972) as any actions that benefit another regardless of the benefits or self sacrifices of the actor.

Altruism is a type of helping/prosocial behaviour that is "voluntary, costly to the altruist and motivated by something other than the expectation of material or social reward" (Walster & Piliavin, 1972).

> *The key difference when distinguishing between these definitions is that prosocial behaviour is that which is valued positively by society and aims to improve a situation whereas altruism is more personal because there is a desire to benefit another individual, derived from perspective taking or empathy.*

Explanations for Altruism/Helping Behaviour

Biological/evolutionary approach

Only by helping others have humans ensured survival. Sometimes altruistic/sacrificial behaviour will occur because it increases the chance of the species/gene pool surviving. Two specific explanations are offered: that of kin selection, where altruism occurs in closest relatives to increase the reproduction of relative genes; and reciprocity among non-relatives, where help is offered to others when costs to the self are low but benefits to the recipient are high. The idea behind this is that others will then reciprocate such help and thus survival is more likely to continue. So, sociobiologists believe that one is biologically predisposed to help others because by doing so one enables one's genes to carry on and this "altruistic gene" must therefore exist since there are no other obvious rewards.

Social learning

This theory believes that helping behaviour is simply learnt through socialisation (being taught what is the correct social behaviour either directly or indirectly, from modelling the behaviour of others). This occurs when helpful behaviour is encouraged in children, is reinforced by offering rewards for altruistic acts and also by observing and then imitating helpful behaviours/attitudes in others. Thus norms/social expectations play an important part in determining altruism, specifically the reciprocity norm where one feels obliged to help those who have, or will, help us, and the social responsibility norm where one learns to offer help to those who are perceived to be in need. Tests have indeed found that personality types who score highly on scales of social responsibility are more likely to be perceived as helpful individuals.

Just world hypothesis

Whether or not we offer help to others may depend on the attribution we make about ourselves, that is, whether one believes one is a helpful person or not, and then act accordingly. Furthermore, attributions about the person in need determine whether or not we will offer help. According to Lerner and Miller's just world hypothesis (1978), people get what they deserve and therefore help will only be offered if one feels this is not the case, such that help is offered to try to remove a perceived injustice.

Mood

Good moods are more likely to produce helpful behaviour as they arouse positive thoughts and activities such as prosocial behaviour. According to Schwarz's affect-as-information model (1990), positive mood tells an individual that an environment is safe and as a result help is more likely to be offered than if it is perceived as dangerous. In contrast, being in a bad mood means that a person becomes more self-focused and is less likely to offer help to others/behave in a prosocial way as a result.

Motivation

Batson (1994) outlines four motives for helping others, including: *egoism*, where help is offered to benefit oneself, to secure material and social rewards and avoid punishment; *altruism*, where help benefits another individual: *collectivism*, where prosocial behaviour aids the welfare of a social group; and *principalism*, where help is offered in order to sustain moral principles.

Handy Hints for Evaluating Explanations for Prosocial Behaviour

If you recall, it is not sufficient just to know the relevant theories, but you also need to be able to think about them critically. You may therefore want to consider the following:

- Do the explanations offered by sociobiologists apply as well to human behaviour as animals, or is it the case that prosocial behaviour in humans is determined by more complex social and cognitive processes in addition to basic biology?
- Is social learning simply a passive process, which means you learn and behave only according to social norms? Could it be that cognitions and social experiences play an equal role in determining our prosocial behaviour?
- Is a belief in a just world sufficient to precipitate helping, or is it the case that help will only be offered when one felt it was possible to completely solve a problem, and therefore truly redress an unjust balance (as believed by Miller, 1977)?
- Since moods are often short-lived, is it surely not too difficult to determine the overall prosocial tendencies of an individual?
- Is it not very hard to separate types of motivation when looking at prosocial behaviour, for example, when one is motivated to help others rather than oneself if the end result is simply to make oneself feel "better"?

REMEMBER

Explanations for Helping

Help is offered because:

➤ It ensures survival of one's genes
➤ Norms learnt in childhood indicate that this is how one should behave
➤ Belief in a just world means that help is offered to maintain a sense of justice
➤ Good mood encourages positive/helping behaviour
➤ Motivation benefits oneself, another individual, group or societies principles

BUT

not one of these explanations is sufficient on its own to explain prosocial behaviour.

Key Thinkers

Batson's empathy arousal (1994)
Recognised that empathy is an emotion consistent with someone else's feelings, it is something that allows us to identify with another's emotions and therefore, according to Batson, one helps others because of empathy, so one identifies with another's distress and is then motivated to help in order to stop this feeling. This process involves perspective taking (seeing someone else's viewpoint), personal distress (feeling emotional) and empathic concern. Help is then offered because it is only by seeing someone else's viewpoint that one "experiences" their feelings and therefore helps.

Latane & Darley's cognitive model (1970)
Examined bystander intervention, which can be described as intervening behaviour offered by those witnessing an emergency. This is because research found that people are actually less likely to help in an emergency situation if in the presence of others (known as the bystander effect). The model suggests that a bystander makes a series of decisions before deciding whether or not to offer help to a victim. This includes initially noticing an event/that someone needs help, interpreting the situation as an emergency, deciding whether or not to assume responsibility, knowing what to do and then implementing a decision.

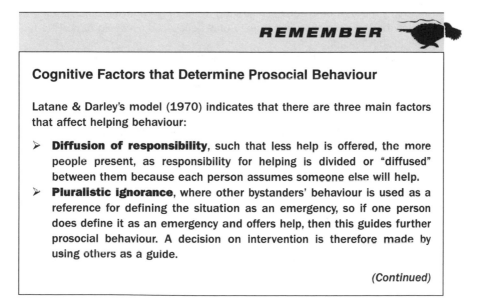

REMEMBER

Cognitive Factors that Determine Prosocial Behaviour

Latane & Darley's model (1970) indicates that there are three main factors that affect helping behaviour:

- ➤ **Diffusion of responsibility**, such that less help is offered, the more people present, as responsibility for helping is divided or "diffused" between them because each person assumes someone else will help.
- ➤ **Pluralistic ignorance**, where other bystanders' behaviour is used as a reference for defining the situation as an emergency, so if one person does define it as an emergency and offers help, then this guides further prosocial behaviour. A decision on intervention is therefore made by using others as a guide.

(Continued)

> (Continued)

> ➢ **Evaluation apprehension**, because the presence of others makes the bystander feel anxious about intervening and they may be less likely to offer help. However, it may also increase prosocial behaviour if the bystander feels competent and uses others as an incentive to demonstrate competence.

Piliavin, Piliavin, Dovido, Gaertner & Clark
bystander-calculus model (1981)

Proposes that bystanders will offer help depending on their level of arousal and on the costs and rewards of potential actions. It involves three stages: experiencing physiological arousal; interpreting and labelling that arousal; and evaluating the consequences (rewards/costs) of offering help. It therefore encompasses the situation, characteristics of the victim and on the cognitive processes involved in decision making. Help is most likely to be offered if it reduces arousal and involves few costs.

Handy Hints for Evaluating the Work of the Key Thinkers

- Empathy may not be a good explanation for helping behaviour because it may simply be the case that people help only because they would otherwise feel bad for not helping.
- The presence of others in the situation is only one of many factors accounting for bystander behaviour and Latane & Darley's model (1970) fails to account for the range of other factors that might influence the decision-making process. The model is therefore too simplistic and does not explain why any of the decisions may be made.
- Not all bystanders either experience arousal or have time to consciously weigh up the rewards and costs of helping in an emergency situation.

Key Research

Batson (1994)

Students watched 'Elaine' receiving mild electric shocks and were then asked to take her place after being told they were either free to leave the room or would have to stay and watch her even if they did not want to substitute themselves. They were all given a placebo drug and misled about its effects so that they would either feel empathic concern or personally distressed. Most of those who felt empathic concern offered to take Elaine's place.

> *This study supports Batson's empathy altruism model because it shows that those students who identified with Elaine were more likely to offer to take her shocks because they felt empathic concern and they did this for unselfish reasons, whereas those experiencing personal distress were only motivated to help for personal reasons such as fear of social disapproval. The study did, however, lack experimental realism and so the results may reflect the fact that participants did not take the situation entirely seriously and behaved in the way that they thought was expected of them (demand characteristics).*

Latane & Darley (1970)
Students were left in a room completing a questionnaire when smoke began to pour in. It was found that 75 per cent of those who were alone in this situation sought help, and this decreased to less than 40 per cent if there were two others present.

Latane & Rodin (1969)
When male participants, left filling in a questionnaire, heard a woman having difficulty opening a filing cabinet, followed by a crash and moaning, they offered help 70 per cent of the time if alone but only 40 per cent of the time if with just one other participant.

Darley & Latane (1968)
Student participants were led to believe that they either were alone with another student (who would later appear to have an epileptic fit) or were accompanied by one or four other students beside the "seizure" victim. Help was offered 85 per cent of the time if the bystander thought they were the only person to help, and this prosocial behaviour decreased the greater the presence of others.

> *This supports the idea that diffusion of responsibility and pluralistic ignorance exist because help was less likely to be offered and was slower to happen when people believed that other potential helpers were present and responsibility therefore diffused. Since the study was, however, carried out in a laboratory, and not in a real-life setting, it lacks ecological validity.*

Piliavin, Rodin & Piliavin (1969)

This study found that how a person was portrayed affected whether or not help was offered. If a victim collapsed on a subway train, they were more likely to be helped if they were perceived to be ill (carrying a cane) rather than drunk (carrying a brown paper bag), and also if the race of the victim matched that of the bystander.

In order to complete an examination question on this topic, you will need to understand how each of these research studies supports a model of prosocial/ bystander behaviour. This has been done for you in a couple of the examples above, but you will need to expand on each example if writing an essay. Doing so will also allow you to check your understanding both of the research and of the theory itself.

Handy Hints for Evaluating Research Studies

- When evaluating studies, the key thing to consider is the research methods used (look back on the section "Basics in Social Psychology").
- Is it suitable to research social behaviour in a laboratory environment or does this lead to unnatural reactions?
- Are the aims of the studies carried out so obvious that the results are simply due to demand characteristics?
- What are the ethical issues involved in recording the reactions of participants who are not aware of their own participation, for example, in Piliavin et al.'s (1969) subway study?

Tasks

1 Complete Table 4 on explanations for, and evaluation of, altruism.

2 Complete Exercise 1 (at the end of this section) on key research on altruism.

3 Go back to each study on bystander intervention and summarise how these studies might provide support for cognitive and bystander-calculus models. Then write a list of bullet points criticising each study using the Handy Hints provided.

"Consider both explanations and research studies relating to altruism/prosocial behaviour."

To answer this question you will need to cover the key definitions involved in this topic such as altruism, empathy/empathic concern, just world belief, prosocial behaviour, social responsibility, and show an understanding of the reasons/ explanations given for helping behaviour including evolutionary/biological explanations, social learning theory, belief in a just world, the influence of mood and types of motivation. Don't forget to add some evaluation – good and bad – of these explanations. You must also be able to describe and evaluate research studies relevant to this area, including Batson's "shock" study, before drawing conclusions about research into this area as a whole.

"Outline and evaluate psychological research into bystander behaviour."

In the course of your essay it should be clear that you understand the key terms bystander effect, bystander intervention, diffusion of responsibility, evaluation apprehension and pluralistic ignorance. You also need to show an awareness of the reasons for bystander behaviour, particularly diffusion of responsibility, pluralistic ignorance and evaluation apprehension, and demonstrate an understanding of cognitive and bystander-calculus models involved in this process. Since the essay title asks you to evaluate, you must consider the strengths and weaknesses of these models and included within this must be the fact that there is some support for their existence as shown in the work of Latane & Darley (smoke experiment), Latane & Rodin (lady in distress study), Darley & Latane (epileptic fit study) and Piliavin et al. (subway study). Remember, however, that these studies can be criticised for their methodology and you should be willing to acknowledge and expand on a discussion of this.

Common Pitfalls

- Do not mix up the key terms prosocial behaviour, altruism and bystander behaviour, as they all have similar meanings but are quite different.
- You must be clear which explanations are relevant to altruism and which are explanations for bystander behaviour, particularly as one focuses on why people do help and the other on why they may not!

- Diffusion of responsibility, pluralistic ignorance and evaluation apprehension are central to research into bystander behaviour, but it is crucial that you relate these specifically to the cognitive model, whilst acknowledging that other models also look at the situation and person variables.
- There are common elements in the supporting studies in that they all seek to support the reasons for helping behaviour, nevertheless they offer different explanations and you must be clear and precise about which experiment supports which explanation – making it clear to your examiner that you understand this and are not just quoting studies with no real idea of their relevance.
- Do not just outline research, but remember to evaluate it – say why it has been useful or what the pitfalls are.

Textbook guide

BATSON, C. D. (1991). *The altruism question. Toward a social-psychological answer.* Hillsdale, NJ: Lawrence Erlbaum. Considers altruism in its historical context.

DARLEY, J. M. & LATANE, B. (1968). Bystander intervention in emergencies: Diffusion of responsibility. *Journal of Personality & Social Psychology, 8,* 377–383.

LATANE, B. & RODIN, J. (1969). A lady in distress: Inhibiting effects of friends and strangers on bystander Intervention. *Journal of Experimental Social Psychology, 5,* 189–202.

PILIAVIN, I., RODIN, J. & PILIAVIN, J. A. (1969). Good Samaritanism: an underground phenomenon? *Journal of Personality & Social Psychology, 13,* 289–299.

SCHROEDER, D. A., PENNER, L. A., DOVIDIO, J. F. & PILIAVIN, J. A. (1995). *The psychology of helping and altruism.* New York: McGraw-Hill. Comprehensive coverage on prosocial behaviour offered.

http://www.socialpsychology.org?social.htm#prosocial Links to research on prosocial behaviour.

Table 4 Explanations and Evaluation of Altruism

	Summary of this explanation	*Evaluation of this explanation*
Biological explanations		
Social learning theory		
Just world hypothesis		
Mood		
Motivation		

EXERCISE 1

Key research on altruism

- Outline Batson's empathy-altruism hypothesis.

- Support for this theory comes from Batson's study where "Elaine" received electric shocks – outline below.

- Evaluate this theory/the strengths and weaknesses of this study.

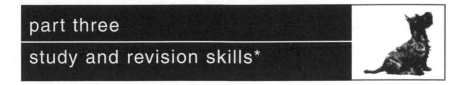

part three

study and revision skills*

*in collaboration with David McIlroy

3.1

introduction

If you work your way carefully through this Part Three you should at the end be better equipped to:

- profit from your lectures;
- benefit from your seminars;
- construct your essays efficiently;
- develop effective revision strategies; and
- respond comprehensively to the pressures of exam situations.

In the five sections that lie ahead you will be presented with:

- checklists and bullet points to focus your attention on key issues;
- exercises to help you participate actively in the learning experience;
- illustrations and analogies to enable you to anchor learning principles in everyday events and experiences;
- worked examples to demonstrate the use of such features as structure, headings and continuity; and
- tips that provide practical advice in nutshell form.

In the exercises that are presented, each student should decide how much effort they would like to invest in each exercise, according to individual preferences and requirements. Some of the points in the exercises will be covered in the text either before or after the exercise. You might prefer to read each section right through before going back to tackle the exercises. Suggested answers are provided in italics after some of the exercises, so avoid these if you prefer to work through the exercises on your own. The aim is to prompt you to reflect on the material, remember what you have read and trigger you to add your own thoughts. Space is provided for you to write your responses down in a few words, or you may prefer to reflect on them within your own mind. However, writing will help you to slow down and digest the material and may also enable you to process the information at a deeper level of learning.

Finally, the overall aim of this Part Three is to point you to the keys for academic and personal development. The twin emphases of academic development and personal qualities are stressed throughout. By giving attention to these factors you will give yourself the toolkit you will need to excel in your psychology course.

3.2	
how to get the most out of your lectures	

This section will enable you to:

- make the most of your lecture notes
- prepare your mind for new terms
- develop an independent approach to learning
- write efficient summary notes from lectures
- take the initiative in building on your lectures

Keeping in Context

According to higher educational commentators and advisors, best quality learning is facilitated when it is set within an overall learning context. It should be the responsibility of your tutors to provide a context for you to learn in, but it is your responsibility to see the overall context, and you can do this even before your first lecture begins. Such a panoramic view can be achieved by becoming familiar with the outline content of both psychology as a subject and the entire study programme. Before you go into each lecture you should briefly remind yourself of where it fits into the overall scheme of things. Think, for example, of how more confident you feel when you move into a new city (for example, to attend university) once you become familiar with your bearings, such as where you live in relation to college, shops, stores, buses, trains, places of entertainment and so on.

> *The same principle applies to your course – find your way around your study programme and locate the position of each lecture within this overall framework.*

Use of Lecture Notes

It is always beneficial to do some preliminary reading before you enter a lecture. If lecture notes are provided in advance (for example, electronically), then print these out, read over them and bring them with you to the lecture. You can insert question marks on issues where you will need further clarification. Some lecturers prefer to provide full notes, some prefer to make skeleton outlines available and some prefer to issue no notes at all. If notes are provided, take full advantage and supplement these with your own notes as you listen. In a later section on memory techniques you will see that humans possess ability for "re-learning savings" – that is, it is easier to learn material the second time round, as it is evident that we have a capacity to hold residual memory deposits. So some basic preparation will equip you with a great advantage; you will be able to "tune in" and think more clearly about the lecture than you would have done with the preliminary work.

> *If you set yourself too many tedious tasks at the early stages of your academic programme, you may lose some motivation and momentum. A series of short, simple, achievable tasks can give your mind the "lubrication" you need. For example, you are more likely to maintain preliminary reading for a lecture if you set modest targets.*

Mastering Technical Terms

Let us assume that in an early lecture you are introduced to a series of new terms such as "paradigm", "empirical" and "ecological validity". If you are hearing these and other terms for the first time, you could end up with a headache! New words can be threatening, especially if you have to face a string of them in one lecture. The uncertainty about the new terms may impair your ability to benefit fully from the lecture and therefore hinder the quality of your learning. Psychology requires technical terms, and the use of them is unavoidable. However, when you have heard a term a number of times it will not seem as daunting as it initially was. It is claimed that individuals may have particular strengths in the scope of their vocabulary. Some people may have a good recognition vocabulary – they immediately know what a word means when they read it or hear it in context. Others have a good command of language when they speak – they have an ability to recall words freely. Still others are more fluent in recall when they write – words seem to flow rapidly for them when they engage in the dynamics of writing. You can work at developing all three approaches in your course, and the checklist below the next paragraph may be of some help in mastering and marshalling the terms you hear in lectures.

In terms of learning new words, it will be very useful if you can first try to work out what they mean from their context when you first encounter them. You might be much better at this than you imagine, especially if there is only one word in the sentence that you do not understand. It would also be very useful if you could obtain a small indexed notebook and use this to build up your own glossary of terms. In this way you could include a definition of a word, an example of its use, where it fits into a theory and any practical application of it.

Checklist: Mastering terms used in your lectures

✓   Read lecture notes before the lectures and list any unfamiliar terms.

✓   Read over the listed terms until you are familiar with their sound.

✓   Try to work out meanings of terms from their context.

✓   Do not suspend learning the meaning of a term indefinitely.

✓   Write out a sentence that includes the new word (do this for each word).

✓   Meet with other students and test each other with the technical terms.

✓   Jot down new words you hear in lectures and check out the meaning soon afterwards.

Your confidence will greatly increase when you begin to follow the flow of arguments that contain technical terms, and more especially when you can freely use the terms yourself in speaking and writing.

Developing Independent Study

In the current educational ethos there are the twin aims of cultivating teamwork/group activities and independent learning. There is not necessarily a conflict between the two, as they should complement each other. For example, if you are committed to independent learning you have more to offer other students when you work in small groups, and you will also be prompted to follow up on the leads given by them. Furthermore, the guidelines given to you in lectures are designed to lead you into deeper independent study. The issues raised in lectures are pointers to provide direction and structure for your extended personal pursuit. Your aim should invariably be to build on what you are given, and you should never think of merely returning the bare bones of the lecture material in a course work essay or exam.

It is always very refreshing to a marker to be given work from a student that contains recent studies that the examiner had not previously encountered.

Note-taking Strategy

Note taking in lectures is an art that you will perfect only with practice and by trial and error. Each student should find the formula that works best for him or her. What works for one does not necessarily work for the other. Some students can write more quickly than others, some are better at shorthand than others and some are better at deciphering their own scrawl! The problem will always be to try to find a balance between concentrating beneficially on what you hear with making sufficient notes that will enable you to comprehend later what you have heard. You should not, however, become frustrated by the fact that you will not understand or remember immediately everything you have heard.

> *By being present at a lecture, and by making some attempt to attend to what you hear, you will already have a substantial advantage over those students who do not attend.*

Checklist: Note-taking in lectures

✓ Develop the note-taking strategy that works best for you.

✓ Work at finding a balance between listening and writing.

✓ Make some use of optimal short hand (for example, a few key words may summarise a story).

✓ Too much writing may impair the flow of the lecture for you.

✓ Too much writing may impair the quality of your notes.

✓ Some limited notes are better than none.

✓ Good note taking may facilitate deeper processing of information.

✓ It is essential to "tidy up" notes as soon as possible after a lecture.

✓ Reading over notes soon after lectures will consolidate your learning.

Developing the Lecture

Some educationalists have criticised the value of lectures because they allege that these are a mode of merely "passive learning". This can certainly be an accurate conclusion to arrive at (that is, if students approach lectures in the wrong way) and lecturers can work to devise ways of making lectures more interactive. For example, they can make use of interactive handouts or by posing questions during the lecture and giving time out for students to reflect on these. Other possibilities are short discussions at given junctures in the lecture or use of small groups within the session. As a student you do not have to enter a lecture in passive mode, and you can ensure that you are not merely a passive recipient of information by taking steps to develop the lecture yourself. A list of suggestions is presented below to help you take the initiative in developing the lecture content.

Checklist: Avoid lecture being a passive Experience

✓ Try to interact with the lecture material by asking questions.
✓ Highlight points that you would like to develop in personal study.
✓ Trace connections between the lecture and other parts of your study programme.
✓ Bring together notes from the lecture and other sources.
✓ Restructure the lecture outline into your own preferred format.
✓ Think of ways in which aspects of the lecture material can be applied.
✓ Design ways in which aspects of the lecture material can be illustrated.
✓ If the lecturer invites questions, make a note of all the questions asked.
✓ Follow up on issues of interest that have arisen from the lecture.

You can contribute to this active involvement in a lecture by engaging with the material before, during and after it is delivered.

EXERCISE

Summarise (and/or add) some factors that would help you fully to capitalise on the benefits of a lecture.

....

....

....

....

....

3.3

how to make the most of seminars

This section will enable you to:

- be aware of the value of seminars
- focus on links to learning
- recognise qualities you can use repeatedly
- manage potential problems in seminars
- prepare yourself adequately for seminars

Not to be Underestimated

Seminars are often optional in a degree programme and sometimes poorly attended because they are underestimated. Some students may be convinced that the lecture is the truly authoritative way to receive quality information. Undoubtedly, lectures play an important role in an academic programme, but seminars have a unique contribution to learning that will complement lectures. Other students may feel that their time would be better spent in personal study. Again, private study is unquestionably essential for personal learning and development, nevertheless you will diminish your learning experience if you neglect seminars. If seminars were to be removed from academic programmes, then something really important would be lost.

Checklist: Some useful features of seminars

✓ Can identify problems that you had not thought of.
✓ Can clear up confusing issues.
✓ Allows you to ask questions and make comments.
✓ Can help you develop friendships and teamwork.

✓ Enables you to refresh and consolidate your knowledge.

✓ Can help you sharpen motivation and redirect study efforts.

An Asset to Complement Other Learning Activities

In higher education at present there is emphasis on variety – variety in delivery, learning experience, learning styles and assessment methods. The seminar is deemed to hold an important place within the overall scheme of teaching, learning and assessment. In some programmes the seminars are directly linked to the assessment task. Whether or not they have such a place in your course, they will provide you with a unique opportunity to learn and develop.

In a seminar you will hear a variety of contributions, and different perspectives and emphases. You will have the chance to interrupt and the experience of being interrupted. You will also learn that you can get things wrong and still survive! It is often the case that when one student admits that they did not know an important piece of information, other students quickly follow on to the same admission in the wake of this. If you can learn to ask questions and not feel stupid, then seminars will give you an asset for learning and a lifelong educational quality.

Creating the Right Climate in Seminars

It has been said that we have been given only one mouth to talk, but two ears to listen. One potential problem with seminars is that some students may take a while to learn this lesson, and other students may have to help hasten them on the way (graciously but firmly!). In lectures your main role is to listen and take notes, but in seminars there is the challenge to strike the balance between listening and speaking. It is important to make a beginning in speaking even if it is just to repeat something that you agree with. You can also learn to disagree in an agreeable way. For example, you can raise a question against what someone else has said and pose this in a good tone, for example, "If that is the case, does that not mean that ..." In addition, it is perfectly possible to disagree with others by avoiding personal attacks, such as, "That was a really stupid thing to say", or "I thought you knew better than that", or "I'm surprised that you don't know that by now". Educationalists say that it is important to have the right climate to learn in, and the avoidance of unnecessary conflict will foster such a climate.

Suggest what can be done to reach agreement (set ground rules) that would help keep seminars running smoothly and harmoniously.

....

....

....

....

....

Some suggestions are: Appoint someone to guide and control the discussion, invite individuals to prepare in advance to make a contribution, hand out agreed discussion questions at some point prior to the seminar, stress at the beginning that no one should monopolise the discussion and emphasise that there must be no personal attacks on any individual (state clearly what this means). Also you could invite and encourage quieter students to participate and assure each person that their contribution is valued.

Links in Learning and Transferable Skills

An important principle in learning to progress from shallow to deep learning is developing the capacity to make connecting links between themes or topics and across subjects. This also applies to the various learning activities, such as lectures, seminars, fieldwork, computer searches and private study. Another factor to think about is, "What skills can I develop, or improve on, from seminars that I can use across my study programme?" A couple of examples of key skills are the ability to communicate and the capacity to work within a team. These are skills that you will be able to use at various points in your course (transferable), but you are not likely to develop them within the formal setting of a lecture.

EXERCISE

Write out or think about (a) three things that give seminars value, and (b) three useful skills that you can develop in seminars.

(a)

✓ ....

✓ ....

✓ ....

(b)

✓ ....

✓ ....

✓ ....

In the above exercises, for (a) you could have: variety of contributors, flexibility to spend more time on problematic issues and agreed agenda settled at the beginning of the seminar. For (b) you could have: communication, conflict resolution and team work.

A key question that you should bring to every seminar is: 'How does this seminar connect with my other learning activities and my assessments?'

An Opportunity to Contribute

If you have never made a contribution to a seminar before, you may need something to use as an "icebreaker". It does not matter if your first contribution is only a sentence or two – the important thing is to make a start. One way to do this is to make brief notes as others contribute, and whilst doing this a question or two might arise in your mind. If your first contribution is a question, that is a good start. Or it may be that you will be able to point out some connection between what others have said, or identify conflicting opinions that need to be resolved. If you have already begun making contributions, it is important that you keep the momentum going, and do not allow yourself to lapse back into the safe cocoon of shyness.

Suggest how you might resolve some of the following problems that might hinder you from making a contribution to seminars.

* One student who dominates and monopolises the discussion.

....

* Someone else has already said what you really want to say.

....

* Fear that someone else will correct you and make you feel stupid.

....

* Feel that your contribution might be seen as short and shallow.

....

* A previous negative experience puts you off making any more contributions.

Strategies for Benefiting from Your Seminar Experience

If you are required to bring a presentation to your seminar, you might want to consult a full chapter on presentations in a complementary study guide (McIlroy, 2003). Alternatively, you may be content with the summary bullet points presented at the end of this section. In order to benefit from discussions in seminars (the focus of this section), some useful summary nutshells are now presented as a checklist.

Checklist: How to benefit from seminars

✓ Do some preparatory reading.
✓ Familiarise yourself with the main ideas to be addressed.
✓ Make notes during the seminar.
✓ Make some verbal contribution, even a question.
✓ Remind yourself of the skills you can develop.
✓ Trace learning links from the seminar to other subjects/topics on your programme.
✓ Make brief bullet points on what you should follow up on.
✓ Read over your notes as soon as possible after the seminar.
✓ Continue discussion with fellow students after the seminar has ended.

If required to give a presentation:

✓ Have a practice run with friends.
✓ If using visuals, do not obstruct them.
✓ Check out beforehand that all equipment works.
✓ Space out points clearly on visuals (large and legible).
✓ Time talk by visuals (for example, 5 slides by 15-minute talk = 3 minutes per slide).
✓ Make sure your talk synchronises with the slide on view at any given point.
✓ Project your voice so that all in the room can hear.
✓ Inflect your voice and do not stand motionless.
✓ Spread eye contact around audience.
✓ Avoid twin extremes of fixed gaze at individuals and never looking at anyone.
✓ Better to fall a little short of time allocation than run over it.
✓ Be selective in what you choose to present.
✓ Map out where you are going and summarise main points at the end.

3.4	
essay writing tips	

This section will enable you to:

- engage quickly with the main arguments
- channel your passions constructively
- note your main arguments in an outline
- find and focus on your central topic questions
- weave quotations into your essay

Getting into the Flow

In essay writing, one of your first aims should be to get your mind active and engaged with your subject. Tennis players like to go out onto the court and hit the ball back and forth just before the competitive match begins. This allows them to judge the bounce of the ball, feel its weight against their racket, get used to the height of the net, the parameters of the court and other factors such as temperature, light, sun and the crowd. In the same way you can "warm up" for your essay by tossing the ideas to and fro within your head before you begin to write. This will allow you to think within the framework of your topic, and this will be especially important if you are coming to the subject for the first time.

The Tributary Principle

A tributary is a stream that runs into a main river as it wends its way to the sea. Similarly, in an essay you should ensure that every idea you introduce is moving toward the overall theme you are addressing. Your idea might, of course, be relevant to a subheading that is in turn relevant to a main heading. Every idea you introduce is to be a "feeder" into the flowing theme. In addition to tributaries, there can also be "distributaries", which are streams that flow away from the river. In an essay these would represent the ideas that run away from the main stream of thought and leave the reader trying to work out what their relevance may have been. It is one thing to have grasped your subject thoroughly, but quite another to convince your reader that this is the case. Your aim should be to build up ideas sentence-by-sentence and paragraph-by-paragraph, until you have communicated your clear purpose to the reader.

> *It is important in essay writing that you not only include material that is relevant, but also make the linking statements that show the connection to the reader.*

Listing and Linking the Key Concepts

Psychology has central concepts that can sometimes be usefully labelled by a single word. Course textbooks may include a glossary of terms and these provide a direct route to the beginning of efficient mastery of the topic. The central words or terms are the essential raw materials that you will need to build upon. Ensure that you learn the words and their definitions, and that you can go on to link the key words together so that in your learning activities you will add understanding to your basic memory work.

It is useful to list your key words under general headings, if that is possible and logical. You may not always see the connections immediately, but when you later come back to a problem that seemed intractable, you will often find that your thinking is much clearer.

Example: Write an essay on "Social Influence"

You might decide to draft your outline points in the following manner (or you may prefer to use a mind map approach):

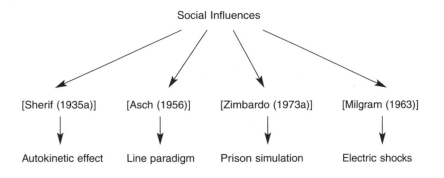

Social Influences

[Sherif (1935a)]   [Asch (1956)]   [Zimbardo (1973a)]   [Milgram (1963)]

Autokinetic effect   Line paradigm   Prison simulation   Electric shocks

An Adversarial System

In higher education, students are required to make the transition from descriptive to critical writing. If you can, think of the critical approach like a law case that is being conducted where there is both a prosecution and a defence. Your concern should be for objectivity, transparency and fairness. No matter how passionately you may feel about a given cause, you must not allow information to be filtered out because of your personal prejudice. An essay is not to become a crusade for a cause in which the contrary arguments are not addressed in an even-handed manner. This means that you should show awareness that opposite views are held, and you should at least represent these as accurately as possible.

Your role as the writer is like that of the judge in that you must ensure that all the evidence is heard, and that nothing will compromise either party.

Stirring Up Passions

The above points do not, of course, mean that you are not entitled to a personal persuasion or to feel passionately about your subject. On the contrary, such feelings may well be a marked advantage if you can bring them under control and channel them into balanced, effective writing (see example below). Some students may be struggling at the other end of the spectrum – being required to write about a topic that they feel quite indifferent about. As you engage with your topic and toss the ideas around in your mind, you will hopefully find that your interest is stimulated, if only at an intellectual level initially. How strongly you feel about a topic, or how much you are interested in it, may depend on whether you choose the topic yourself or whether it has been given to you as an obligatory assignment.

> *It is important in a large project (such as a dissertation) that you choose a topic for which you can maintain your motivation, momentum and enthusiasm.*

Example: An issue that may stir up passions

Arguments for and against the view that social psychological studies are unethical:

For:

- People were deceived.
- They were misinformed about the effects the studies might have.
- Participants in Milgram's study were put under undue pressure when believing they were shocking people.

Against:

- Social knowledge could not advance without the input of these studies.
- When questioned afterwards, most participants were glad they had taken part in the research.
- Debriefing counteracted any ill effects.

Structuring an Outline

Whenever you sense a flow of inspiration to write on a given subject, it is essential to put this into a structure that will allow your inspiration to be communicated clearly. It is a basic principle in all walks of life that structure and order facilitate good communication. Therefore, once you have the flow of inspiration in your essay, you must get this into a structure that will allow the marker to recognise the true quality of your work. For example, you might plan for an introduction, conclusion, three main headings and each of these with several subheadings (see example below). Moreover, you may decide not to include your headings in your final presentation – that is, just use them initially to structure and balance your arguments. Once you have drafted this outline, you can then easily sketch an introduction, and you will have been well prepared for the conclusion when you arrive at that point.

> *A good structure will help you to balance the weight of each of your arguments against each other, and arrange your points in the order that will facilitate the fluent progression of your argument.*

Example: Write an essay that compares and contrasts theories of the self

1 *Similarities between theories*

   a. Agreed social and personal identities
   b. Consideration of individual centred approach

2 *Differences between theories*

   a. Focus on cognitions – self-perception theory
   b. Focus on social context – social comparison, self-categorisation

Finding Major Questions

When you are constructing a draft outline for an essay or project, you should ask what is the major question or questions you wish to address. It would be useful to make a list of all the issues that spring to mind that you might wish to tackle. The ability to design a good question is an art form that should be cultivated, and such questions will allow you to impress your assessor with the quality of your thinking.

> *If you construct your ideas around key questions, this will help you focus your mind and engage effectively with your subject. Your role will be like that of a detective – exploring the evidence and investigating the findings.*

To illustrate the point, consider the example presented below. If you were asked to write an essay on studies of social influence and the resemblance of such processes in the real world, you could focus on experimental validity and ask yourself:

- Did participants believe the authority of the researcher?
- If participants believed the situation to be real, were they giving real electric shocks?
- Did those in Asch's experiment really believe they were giving an honest answer or did they simply believe they were being "set up"?
- Were those acting as prisoners in Zimbardo's study simply behaving as they thought was expected of them?

Rest Your Case

It should be your aim to give the clear impression that your arguments are not based entirely on hunches, bias, feelings or intuition. In exams and essay questions it is usually assumed (even if not directly specified) that you will appeal to evidence to support your claims. Therefore, when you write your essay you should ensure that it is liberally sprinkled with research evidence. By the time the assessor reaches the end of your work, he or she should be convinced that your conclusions are evidence based. A fatal flaw to be avoided is to make claims for which you have provided no authoritative source.

> Give the clear impression that what you have asserted is derived from recognised sources (including up to date). It also looks impressive if you spread your citations across your essay rather than compressing them into a paragraph or two at the beginning and end.

Example: How to introduce evidence and sources

According to O'Neil (1999) ...
Wilson (2003) has concluded that ...
Taylor (2004) found that ...
It has been claimed by McKibben (2002) that ...
Appleby (2001) asserted that ...
A review of the evidence by Lawlor (2004) suggests that ...
Findings from a meta-analysis presented by Rea (2003) would indicate that ...

It is sensible to vary the expression used so that you are not monotonous and repetitive, and it also aids variety to introduce researchers' names at various places in the sentence (not always at the beginning). It is advisable to choose the expression that is most appropriate – for example, you can make a stronger statement about reviews that have identified recurrent and predominant trends in findings as opposed to one study that appears to run contrary to all the rest.

Credit is given for the use of caution and discretion when this is clearly needed.

Careful Use of Quotations

Although it is desirable to present a good range of cited sources, it is not judicious to present these as "patchwork quilt" – that is, you just paste together what others have said with little thought for interpretative comment or coherent structure. It is a good general point to aim to avoid very lengthy quotes – short ones can be very effective. Aim also at blending the quotations as naturally as possible into the flow of your sentences. It is good to vary your practices – sometimes use short, direct, brief quotes (cite page number as well as author and year), and at times you can summarise the gist of a quote in your own words. In this case you should cite the author's name and year of publication but leave out quotation marks and page number.

Use your quotes and evidence in a manner that demonstrates that you have thought the issues through, and have integrated them in a manner that shows you have been focused and selective in the use of your sources.

In terms of referencing, practice may vary from one discipline to the next, but some general points that will go a long way in contributing to good practice are:

- If a reference is cited in the text, it must be in the list at the end (and vice-versa).
- Names and dates in text should correspond exactly with the list in References or Bibliography.

- List of References and Bibliography should be in alphabetical order by the surname (not the initials) of the author or first author.
- Any reference you make in the text should be traceable by the reader (they should clearly be able to identify and trace the source).

A Clearly Defined Introduction

In an introduction to an essay you have the opportunity to define the problem or issue that is being addressed and to set it within context. Resist the temptation to elaborate on any issue at the introductory stage. For example, think of a music composer who throws out hints and suggestions of the motifs that the orchestra will later develop. What he or she does in the introduction is to provide little tasters of what will follow in order to whet the audience's appetite. If you go back to the analogy of the game of tennis, you can think of the introduction as marking out the boundaries of the court in which the game is to be played.

If you leave the introduction and definition of your problem until the end of your writing, you will be better placed to map out the directions that will be taken.

EXERCISE

Look back at the drafted outline on writing an essay on studies of social influence and the resemblance of such processes in the real world. Design an introduction for that essay in about three or four sentences.

Sample Answer – Social influence is where people are influenced by others such that they try to display the attitude or behaviour of the social group, by obeying or conforming to the majority or minority. It occurs because of a desire to be liked or the desire to be right (normative and informational social influence). Several studies can be considered including Asch, Zimbardo and Milgram, and the issues of ecological and experimental validity are important ones.

Conclusion – Adding the Finishing Touches

In the conclusion you should aim to tie your essay together in a clear and coherent manner. It is your last chance to leave an overall impression in your reader's mind. Therefore, you will at this stage want to do justice to your efforts and not sell yourself short. This is your opportunity to identify where the strongest evidence points or where the balance of probability lies. The conclusion to an exam question often has to be written hurriedly under the pressure of time, but with an essay (course work) you have time to reflect on, refine and adjust the content to your satisfaction. It should be your goal to make the conclusion a smooth finish that does justice to the range of content in summary and succinct form. Do not underestimate the value of an effective conclusion. "Sign off" your essay in a manner that brings closure to the treatment of your subject.

> The conclusion facilitates the chance to demonstrate where the findings have brought us to date, to highlight the issues that remain unresolved and to point to where future research should take us.

Top-down and Bottom-up Clarity

An essay gives you the opportunity to refine each sentence and paragraph on your word processor. Each sentence is like a tributary that leads into the stream of the paragraph that in turn leads into the mainstream of the essay. From a "top-down" perspective (that is, starting at the top with your major outline points), clarity is facilitated by the structure you draft in your outline. You can ensure that the subheadings are appropriately placed under the most relevant main heading, and that both sub and main headings are arranged in logical sequence. From a "bottom-up" perspective (that is, building up the details that "flesh out" your main points), you should check that each sentence is a "feeder" for the predominant concept in a given paragraph. When all this is done, you can check that the transition from one point to the next is smooth rather than abrupt.

Checklist: Summary for essay writing

✓ Before you start, have a "warm up" by tossing the issues around in your head.
✓ List the major concepts and link them in fluent form.
✓ Design a structure (outline) that will facilitate balance, progression, fluency and clarity.

✓ Pose questions and address them in critical fashion.

✓ Demonstrate that your arguments rest on evidence and spread cited sources across your essay.

✓ Provide an introduction that sets the scene and a conclusion that rounds off the arguments.

EXERCISE

Write (or at least think about) some additional features that would help facilitate good essay writing.

....

....

....

....

....

In the above checklist you could have features such as originality, clarity in sentence and paragraph structure, applied aspects, addressing a subject you feel passionately about and the ability to avoid going off on a tangent.

3.5 ## revision hints and tips	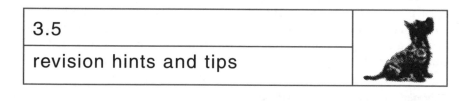

This section will enable you to:

- map out your accumulated material for revision
- choose summary tags to guide your revision
- keep well-organised folders for revision

- make use of effective memory techniques
- develop revision that combines bullet points and in-depth reading
- profit from the benefits of revising with others
- attend to the practical exam details that will help keep panic at bay
- use strategies that keep you task-focused during the exam
- select and apply relevant points from your prepared outlines

The Return Journey

In a return journey you will usually pass by all the same places that you had already passed when you were outward bound. If you had observed the various landmarks on your outward journey, you would be likely to remember them on your return. Similarly, revision is a means to "revisit" what you have encountered before. Familiarity with your material can help reduce anxiety, inspire confidence and fuel motivation for further learning and good performance.

If you are to capitalise on your revision period, then you must have your materials arranged and at hand for the time when you are ready to make your "return journey" through your notes.

Start at the Beginning

Strategy for revision should be on your mind from your first lecture at the beginning of your academic semester. You should be like the squirrel that stores up nuts for the winter. Do not waste any lecture, tutorial, seminar, group discussion and so on by letting the material evaporate into thin air. Get into the habit of making a few guidelines for revision after each learning activity. Keep a folder, or file or little notebook that is reserved for revision and write out the major points that you have learned. By establishing this regular practice you will find that what you have learned becomes consolidated in your mind, and you will also be in a better position to "import" and "export" your material both within and across subjects.

If you do this regularly and do not make the task too tedious, you will be amazed at how much useful summary material you have accumulated when revision time comes.

Compile Summary Notes

It would be useful and convenient to have a little notebook or cards on which you can write outline summaries that provide you with an overview of your subject at a glance. You could also use "treasury tags" to hold different batches of cards together whilst still allowing for inserts and re-sorting. Such practical resources can easily be slipped into your pocket or bag and produced when you are on the bus or train or whilst sitting in a traffic jam. They would also be useful if you are standing in a queue or waiting for someone who is not in a rush! A glance over your notes will consolidate your learning and will also activate your mind to think further about your subject. Therefore it would also be useful to make notes of the questions that you would like to think about in greater depth. Your primary task is to get into the habit of constructing outline notes that will be useful for revision, and a worked example is provided below.

> There is a part of the mind that will continue to work on problems when you have moved on to focus on other issues. Therefore, if you feed on useful, targeted information your mind will continue to work on "automatic pilot" after you have "switched off".

Example: Outline revision structure for attribution study

1 *Key thinkers/theories*

- Rotter – internal and external attribution
- Heider – Naïve psychology
- Jones & Davis – correspondent inference theory
- Kelly – covariation model
- Weiner – attribution theory
- Schacter – emotional ability
- Bem – self-perception

2 *Evaluation of these theories*

- Correspondent inference theory – ignores past behaviour/ stereotypes
- Covariation model – notice most salient features only, do not have accurate facts

- Attribution theory – role of individual differences
- Emotional lability – methodological difficulties

3 *Biases*

- Fundamental attribution error
- Actor-observer effect
- False consensus effect
- Self-serving bias

Keep Organised Records

People who have a fulfilled career have usually developed the twin skills of time and task management. It is worth pausing to remember that you can use your academic training to prepare for your future career in this respect. Therefore, ensure that you do not fall short of your potential because these qualities have not been cultivated. One important tactic is to keep a folder for each subject and divide this topic by topic. You can keep your topics in the same order in which they are presented in your course lectures. Bind them together in a ring binder or folder and use subject dividers to keep them apart. Make a numbered list of the contents at the beginning of the folder, and list each topic clearly as it marks a new section in your folder. Another important practice is to place all your notes on a given topic within the appropriate section and don't put off this simple task, do it straight away. Notes may come from lectures, seminars, tutorials, Internet searches, personal notes and so on. It is also essential when you remove these for consultation that you return them to their "home" immediately after use.

> *Academic success has as much to do with good organisation and planning as it has to do with ability. The value of the quality material you have accumulated on your academic programme may be diminished because you have not organised it into an easily retrievable form.*

Example: an organised record of a history of romantic relationships

- Physical features my girl friends/boy friends have shared or differed in.
- Common and diverse personality characteristics.
- Shared and contrasting interests.

- Frequency of dates with each.
- Places frequented together.
- Contact with both circles of friends.
- Use of humour in our communication.
- Frequency and resolution of conflicts.
- Mutual generosity.
- Courtesy and consideration.
- Punctuality.
- Dress and appearance.

In this fun example, let us imagine that you had five girl friends/boy friends over the last few years. Each of the five names could be included under all of the above subjects. You could then compare them with each other, looking at what they had in common and how they differed. Moreover, you could think of the ones you liked best and least, then look through your dossier to establish why this might have been. You could also judge who had most and least in common with you and whether you are more attracted to those who differed most from you. The questions open to you can go on and on. The real point here is that you will have gathered a wide variety of material that is organised in such a way that will allow you to use a range of evidence to draw some satisfactory and authoritative conclusions – if that is possible in matters so directly related to the heart!

Use Past Papers

Revision will be very limited if it is confined to memory work. You should by all means read over your revision cards or notebook and keep the picture of the major facts in front of your mind's eye. It is also, how-ever, essential that you become familiar with previous exam papers so that you will have some idea of how the questions are likely to be framed. Therefore, build up a good range of past exam papers (especially recent ones) and add these to your folder. Think of cows and sheep; when they have grazed, they lie down and "chew the cud". That is, they regurgitate what they have eaten and take time to digest the food thoroughly.

If you think over previous exam questions, this will help you to not only recall what you have deposited in your memory, but also develop your understanding of the issues. The questions from past exam papers, and further questions that you have developed yourself, will allow you to "chew the cud".

*Example: Evaluate psychological research
into bystander behaviour*

Immediately you can see that you will require two lists, so you can begin to work on documenting your reasons under each as below:

Support: Say how each of these studies supports theories of bystander behaviour

- Latane & Darley – smoke experiment
- Latane & Rodin – lady in distress
- Darley & Latane – epileptic study
- Piliavin – subway study

Criticisms: Say how each of the following criticises the theory/study

- Do these studies have ecological validity, and if so are they like real-life social processes?
- Were the aims of the studies sufficiently obvious that the results are simply due to demand characteristics?
- What are the ethical issues involved in these studies?

You will have also noticed that the word "evaluate" is in the question – so your mind must go to work on making judgements. You may decide to work through problems first and then through pleasures, or it may be your preference to compare point by point as you go along. Whatever conclusion you come to may be down to personal subjective preference, but at least you will have worked through all the issues from both standpoints. The lesson is to ensure that part of your revision should include critical thinking as well as memory work.

> You cannot think adequately without the raw materials provided by your memory deposits.

Employ Effective Mnemonics (Memory Aids)

The Greek word from which "mnemonics" is derived refers to a tomb – a structure that is built in memory of a loved one, friend or respected person. "Mnemonics" can be simply defined as aids to memory – devices that will help you recall information that might otherwise be difficult to retrieve from memory. For example, if you find an old toy in the attic of your house, it may suddenly trigger a flood of childhood memories associated with it. Mnemonics can therefore be thought of as keys that open the memory's storehouse.

Visualisation is one technique that can be used to aid memory. For example, the location method is where a familiar journey is visualised and you can "place" the facts that you wish to remember at various landmarks along the journey, such as a bus stop, a car park, a shop, a store, a bend, a police station, a traffic light and so on. This has the advantage of making an association of the information you have to learn with other material that is already firmly embedded and structured in your memory. Therefore, once the relevant memory is activated, a dynamic "domino effect" will be triggered. However, there is no reason why you cannot use a whole toolkit of mnemonics. Some examples and illustrations of these are presented below.

If you can arrange your subject matter in a logical sequence, this will ensure that your series of facts will also connect with each other and one will trigger the other in recall.

You can use memory devices either at the stage of initial learning or when you later return to consolidate.

Example: Location method

Visualisation
Turn information into pictures, for example, the problems and pleasures of pets could be envisaged as two tug-of-war teams that pull against each other. You could visualise each player as an argument and have the label written on his or her T-shirt. The war could start with two players and then be joined by another two and so on. In addition, you could compare each player's weight to the strength of each argument. You might also want to make use of colour – your favourite colour for the winning team and the colour you dislike most for the losers!

Alliteration's artful aid
Find a series of words that all begin with the same letter. See the example below related to the experiments of Ebbinghaus.

Peg system
"Hang" information onto a term so that when you hear the term you will remember the ideas connected with it (an umbrella term). For example,

in aggression there are different examples – biological, chronological, sociological and psychological. Under biological you could remember "psychodynamic" and "ethological".

Hierarchical system

This is a development of the previous point with higher order, middle order and lower order terms. For example, you could think of the continents of the world (higher order), then group these into the countries under them (middle order). Under countries you could have cities, rivers and mountains (lower order).

Acronyms

Take the first letter of all the key words and make a word from these.

Mind maps

These have become very popular – they allow you to draw lines that stretch out from the central idea and to develop the subsidiary ideas in the same way. It is a little like the pegging and hierarchical methods combined and turned sideways. The method has the advantage of giving you the complete picture at a glance, although they can become a complex work of art!

Rhymes and Chimes

These are words that rhyme and words that end with a similar sound (for example, commemoration, celebration, anticipation). They provide another dimension to memory work by including sound. Memory can be enhanced when information is processed in various modalities, for example, hearing, seeing, speaking, visualising.

A Confidence Booster

At the end of the 19th century, Ebbinghaus and his assistant memorised lists of nonsense words (could not be remembered by being attached to meaning), and then endeavoured to recall these. What they discovered was:

- Some words could be recalled freely from memory, while others appeared to be forgotten.
- Words that could not be recalled were later recognised as belonging to the lists (that is, were not new additions).

- When the lists were jumbled into a different sequence, the experimenters were able to re-jumble them into the original sequence.
- When the words that were "forgotten" were learned again, the learning process was much easier the second time (that is, there was evidence of re-learning savings).

The four points of this experiment can be remembered by alliteration: Recall, Recognition, Reconstruction and Re-learning savings. This experiment has been described as a confidence booster because it demonstrates that memory is more powerful than is often imagined, especially when we consider that Ebbinghaus and his assistant did not have the advantage of processing the meaning of the words.

Alternate Between Methods

It is not sufficient to present outline points in response to an exam question (although it is better to do this than nothing if you have run out of time in your exam). Your aim should be to put "meat on the bones" by adding substance, evidence and arguments to your basic points. You should work at finding the balance between the two methods – outline revision cards might be best reserved for short bus journeys, whereas extended reading might be better employed for longer revision slots at home or in the library. Your ultimate goal should be to bring together an effective, working approach that will enable you to face your exam questions comprehensively and confidently.

> In revision it is useful to alternate between scanning over your outline points and reading through your notes, articles, chapters and so on in an in-depth manner. Also, the use of different times, places and methods will provide you with the variety that might prevent monotony and facilitate freshness.

Example: Outline for a course on social psychology

Your major outline topics might be:

- The self
- Social cognition

- Attribution
- Attitudes and attitude change
- Social influence
- Group processes
- Prejudice and discrimination
- Interpersonal attraction
- Aggressive behaviour
- Prosocial behaviour

This outline would be your overall, bird's-eye view of the course. You could then choose one of the topics and have all your key terms under that. For example, under "prosocial" you might have listed: altruism, Batson's empathy altruism hypothesis, bystander behaviour, cognitive model of bystander behaviour, diffusion of responsibility, evaluation apprehension, Piliavin's bystander calculus model, pluralistic ignorance.

> *If you alternate between memory work and reading, you will soon be able to think through the processes by just looking at your outlines.*

Revising with Others

If you can find a few other students to revise with, this will provide another fresh approach to the last stages of your learning. First ensure that others carry their workload and are not merely using the hard work of others as a short-cut to success. You should think of group sessions as one of the strings on your violin, but not the only string. This collective approach would allow you to assess your strengths and weaknesses (showing you where you are off track), and to benefit from the resources and insights of others. Before you meet up you can each design some questions for the whole group to address. The group could also go through past exam papers and discuss the points that might provide an effective response to each question. It should not be the aim of the group to provide standard and identical answers for each group member to mimic. Groupwork is currently deemed to be advantageous by educationalists, and teamwork is held to be a desirable employability quality.

Each individual should aim to use their own style and content whilst drawing on and benefiting from the group's resources.

EXERCISE

Make a list of the advantages and disadvantages of revising in small groups.

Advantages: Disadvantages:

1. ....…   ....…

2. ....…   ....…

3. ....…   ....…

4. ....…   ....…

5. ....…   ....…

Can the disadvantages be eliminated, or at least minimised?

Checklist: Good study habits for revision time

✓ Set a date for the "official" beginning of revision and prepare for "revision mode".

✓ Do not force cramming by leaving revision too late.

✓ Take breaks from revision to avoid saturation.

✓ Indulge in relaxing activities to give your mind a break from pressure.

✓ Minimise or eliminate use of alcohol during the revision season.

✓ Get into a good rhythm of sleep to allow renewal of your mind.

✓ Avoid excessive caffeine, especially at night so that sleep is not disrupted.

✓ Try to adhere to regular eating patterns.

✓ Try to have a brisk walk in fresh air each day (for example, in the park).

✓ Avoid excessive dependence on junk food and snacks.

EXERCISE

Write your own checklist on what to add to the revision process to ensure that it does not become just a memory exercise.

....

....

....

....

....

In the above exercise, what you could add to memory work during revision might include: using past exam papers; setting problem-solving tasks; doing drawings to show connections and directions between various concepts; explaining concepts to student friends in joint revision sessions; devising your own mock exam questions.

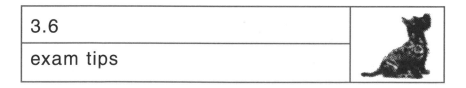

3.6	
exam tips	

This section will enable you to:

- develop strategies for controlling your nervous energy
- tackle worked examples of time and task management in exams
- attend to the practical details associated with the exam
- stay focused on the exam questions
- link revision outlines to strategy for addressing exam questions

Handling Your Nerves

Exam nerves are not unusual and it has been concluded that test anxiety arises because of the perception that your performance is being evaluated, that the consequences are likely to be serious and that you are working under the pressure of a time restriction. However, it has also been asserted that the activation of the autonomic nervous system is adaptive in that it is designed to prompt us to take action in order to avoid danger. If you focus on the task at hand rather than on feeding a downward negative spiral in your thinking patterns, this will help you to keep your nerves under control. In the run up to your exams, you can practice some simple relaxation techniques that will help you bring stress under control.

> *It is a very good thing if you can interpret your nervous reactions positively, but the symptoms are more likely to be problematic if you interpret them negatively, pay too much attention to them or allow them to interfere with your exam preparation or performance.*

Practices that may help reduce or buffer the effects of exam stress are:

- listening to music
- going for a brisk walk
- simple breathing exercises
- some muscle relaxation
- watching a movie
- enjoying some laughter
- doing some exercise
- relaxing in a bath (with music if preferred).

The best choice is going to be the one (or combination) that works best for you – perhaps to be discovered by trial and error. Some of the above techniques can be practised on the morning of the exam, and even the memory of them can be used just before the exam. For example, you could run over a relaxing tune in your head and have this echo inside you as you enter the exam room. The idea behind all this is, first, stress levels must come down, and second, relaxing thoughts will serve to displace stressful reactions. It has been said that stress is the body's call to take action, but anxiety is a maladaptive response to that call.

> *It is important to be convinced that your stress levels can come under control, and that you can have a say in this. Do not give anxiety a vacuum to work in.*

Time Management with Examples

The all-important matter as you approach an exam is to develop the belief that you can take control over the situation. As you work through the list of issues that you need to address, you will be able to tick them off one by one. One of the issues you will need to be clear about before the exam is the length of time you should allocate to each question. Sometimes this can be quite simple (although it is always necessary to read the rubric carefully), for example, if two questions are to be answered in a two-hour paper, you should allow one hour for each question. If it is a two-hour paper with one essay question and five shorter answers, you could allow one hour for the essay and 12 minutes each for the shorter questions. However, you always need to check out the weighting for the marks on each question, and you will also need to deduct whatever time it takes you to read over the paper and to choose your questions. Work out a time management strategy in the excercise below. More importantly, give yourself some practice on the type of papers you are likely to face.

Remember to check if the structure of your exam paper is the same as in previous years, and do not forget that excessive time on your "strongest" question may not compensate for very poor answers to other questions. Also ensure that you read the rubric carefully in the exam.

EXERCISE

Working out the division of exam labour by time.

1. A 3-hour paper with four compulsory questions (equally weighted in marks).

2. A 3-hour paper with two essays and ten short questions (each of the three sections carry one-third of the marks).

3. A 2-hour paper with two essay questions and 100 multiple-choice questions (half marks are on the two essays and half marks on the multiple choice section).

Get into the calculating frame of mind and be sure to have the calculations done before starting the exam. Ensure that the structure of the exam has not changed since the last one. Also deduct the time taken to read over the paper in allocating time to each question.

Suggested answers to previous exercise:

1 *This allows 45 minutes for each question (4 questions × 45 minutes = 2 hours). However, if you allow 40 minutes for each question, this will give you 20 minutes (4 questions × 5 minutes) to read over the paper and plan your outlines.*
2 *In this example you can spend 1 hour on each of the two major questions, and 1 hour on the ten short questions. For the two major questions you could allow 10 minutes for reading and planning on each, and 50 minutes for writing. In the ten short questions, you could allow 6 minutes in total for each (10 questions × 6 minutes = 60 minutes). However, if you allow approximately 1 minute reading and planning time, this will allow 5 minutes writing time for each question.*
3 *In this case you have to divide 120 minutes by three questions – this allows 40 minutes for each. You could, for example, allow 5 minutes reading/planning time for each essay and 35 minutes for writing (or 10 minutes reading/planning and 30 minutes writing). After you have completed the two major questions you are left with 40 minutes to tackle the 100 multiple-choice questions.*

You may not be able to achieve total precision in planning time for tasks, but you will have a greater feeling of control and confidence if you have some reference points to guide you.

Task Management with Examples

After you have decided on the questions you wish to address, you then need to plan your answers. Some students prefer to plan all outlines and draft work at the beginning, whilst others prefer to plan and address one answer before proceeding to address the next question. Decide on your strategy before you enter the exam room, and stick to your plan. When you have done your draft outline as rough work, you should allocate an appropriate time for each section. This will prevent you from excessive treatment of some aspects, whilst falling short on other parts. Such careful planning will help you to achieve balance, fluency and symmetry.

Keep awareness of time limitations; this will help you to write succinctly, keep focused on the task and prevent you dressing up your responses with unnecessary padding.

Some students put as much effort into their rough work as they do into their exam essay.

> An over-elaborate mind map may give the impression that the essay is little more than a repetition of this detailed structure, and that the quality of the content has suffered because too much time was spent on the plan.

EXERCISE

Work the time allocation for the following outline, allowing for one hour on the question. Deduct 10 minutes taken at the beginning for choice and planning.

Discuss theories of attitude change

1. *Cognitive dissonance*

    (a) Inconsistency leads to change, brought about by effort justification, induced compliance and free choice.
    (b) Supported by Festinger and Carlsmith.
    (c) Criticisms of model.

2. *Elaboration likelihood model*

    (a) Persuasion leads to attitude change, much effort = central route, little effort = peripheral route.
    (b) Support for model.
    (c) Criticisms of model.

Attend to Practical Details

This short section is designed to remind you of the practical details that should be attended to in preparation for an exam. There are always students who turn up late, or to the wrong venue or for the wrong exam, or do not turn up at all! Check and re-check that you have all the details of each exam correctly noted. What you don't need is to arrive late and then have to tame your panic reactions. The exam season is the time when you should aim to be at your best.

Turn up to the right venue in good time so that you can quieten your mind and bring your stress under control.

Make note of the details in the checklist below and ensure that you have taken control of each one.

Checklist: Practical exam details

✓ Check that you have the correct venue.

✓ Make sure you know how to locate the venue before the exam day.

✓ Ensure that the exam time you have noted is accurate.

✓ Allow sufficient time for your journey and consider the possibility of delays.

✓ Bring an adequate supply of stationary including spare items such as pens etc.

✓ Bring a watch for your time and task management.

✓ You may need some liquid, such as a small bottle of still water.

✓ You may also need to bring some tissues.

✓ Observe whatever exam regulations your university/college has set in place.

✓ Fill in required personal details before the exam begins.

Control Wandering Thoughts

In a simple study conducted in the 1960s, Ganzer found that students who frequently lifted their heads and looked away from their scripts during exams tended to perform poorly. This makes sense because it implies that the students were taking too much time out when they should have been on task. *One way to fail your exam is to get up and walk out of the test room, but another way is to "leave" the test room mentally by being preoccupied with distracting thoughts.* The distracting thoughts may be either related to the exam itself or totally irrelevant to it. The net effect of both these forms of intrusion is to distract you from the task at hand and debilitate your test performance. Read over the two lists of distracting thoughts presented below.

Typical test-relevant thoughts (evaluative):

• I wish I had prepared better.
• I wonder what will the examiner think.

- Others are doing better than me.
- What I am writing is nonsense.
- Can't remember important details.

Characteristic test-irrelevant thoughts (non-evaluative):

- looking forward to this weekend.
- Which video should I watch tonight?
- His remark really annoyed me yesterday!
- Wonder how the game will go on Saturday?
- I wonder if he/she really likes me?

Research has consistently shown that distracting, intrusive thoughts during an exam are more detrimental to performance than stressful symptoms such as sweaty palms, dry mouth, tension, trembling and so on. Moreover, it does not matter whether the distracting thoughts are negative evaluations related to the exam or are totally irrelevant to the exam. The latter may be a form of escape from the stressful situation.

Checklist: Practical suggestions for controlling wandering thoughts

✓ Be aware that this problem is detrimental to performance.

✓ Do not look around to find distractions.

✓ If distracted, write down "keep focused on task".

✓ If distracted again, look back at above and continue to do this.

✓ Start to draft rough work as soon as you can.

✓ If you struggle with initial focus, then re-read or elaborate on your rough work.

✓ If you have commenced your essay, re-read you last paragraph (or two).

✓ Do not throw fuel on your distracting thoughts – starve them by re-engaging with the task at hand.

Links to Revision

If you have followed the guidelines given for revision, you will be well equipped with outline plans when you enter the exam room. You may have chosen to use headings and subheadings, mind maps, hierarchical approaches or just a series of simple mnemonics. Whatever method you choose to use, you should be furnished with a series of memory triggers that will open the treasure house door for you once you begin to write.

Although you may have clear templates with a definite structure or framework for organising your material, you will need to be flexible about how this should be applied to your exam questions.

Example: How to use memory triggers

Imagine that attitudes are one of the topics that you will be examined on. You decide to memorise lists of attitudes.

Attitude formation:

- Behavioural – direct experience, conditioning, observation.
- Cognitive – information integration, self-perception, mood-as-information, heuristics, persuasion.

Relationship between attitudes and behaviour:

- Compatability
- Aggregation
- Strength
- Expectancy value models

Key thinkers/attitude change:

- Cognitive dissonance (Festinger)
- Elaboration likelihood model (Petty & Cacioppo)
- Heuristic systematic model (Chaiken)

Measurement:

- Thurstone
- Likert scale
- Semantic differential scale
- Sociometry
- Scalogram

The basic mental template might be these and a few other categories. You know that you will not need every last detail, although you may need to select a few from each category. For example, you might be asked to discuss:

- psychologists' attempts to change people's attitudes;
- the relationship between attitudes and behaviour;
- attitude formation; or
- theories of attitude change.

Restrict your material to what is relevant to the question, but bear in mind that this may allow you some scope.

The Art of "Name Dropping"

In most topics at university you will be required to cite studies as evidence for your arguments and to link these to the names of researchers, scholars or theorists. It will help if you can use the correct dates, or at least the decades, and it is good to demonstrate that you have used contemporary sources and have done some independent work. A marker will have dozens if not hundreds of scripts to work through and they will know if you are just repeating the same phrases from the same sources as every one else. There is inevitably a certain amount of this that must go on, but there is room for you to add fresh and original touches that demonstrate independence and imagination.

Give the clear impression that you have done more than the bare minimum and that you have enthusiasm for the subject. Also, spread the use of researchers' names across your exam essay rather than compressing them into, for example, the first and last paragraphs.

Flight, Fight or Freeze

As previously noted, the autonomic nervous system (ANS) is activated when danger or apparent danger is imminent. Of course the threat does not have to be physical, as in the case of an exam, a job interview, a driving test or a television appearance. Indeed, the ANS can be activated even at the anticipation of a future threat. However, the reaction is more likely to be stronger as you enter into the crucial time of testing or challenge. Symptoms may include deep breathing, trembling, headaches, nausea, tension, dry mouth and palpitations. How should we react to these once they have been triggered? A postman might decide to run away from a barking dog and run the risk of being chased and bitten. A second possible response is to freeze on the spot – this might arrest the animal in its tracks, but is no use in an exam situation. In contrast, to fight might not be the best strategy against the dog, but will be more productive in an exam. That is, you are going into the exam room to "tackle" the questions, and not to run away from the challenge before you.

The final illustration below uses the analogy of archery to demonstrate how you might take control in an exam.

Example: Lessons from archery

- Enter the exam room with a quiver full of arrows – all the points you will need to use.
- Eye up the target board you are to shoot at – choose the exam questions.
- Stand in good position for balance and vision – prepare your time management.
- Prepare your bow and arrow and take aim at the target – keep focused on the task at hand and do not be sidetracked.
- Pull the string of the bow back to get maximum thrust on the arrow – match your points to the appropriate question.
- Aim to hit the board where the best marks are (bull's-eye or close) – do not be content with the minimum standard such as a mere pass.
- Pull out arrows and shoot one after another to gain maximum hits and advantage – do not be content with preparing just one or two strong points.
- Make sure your arrows are sharp and the supporting bow and string are firm – choose relevant points and support with evidence.
- Avoid wasted effort by loose and careless shots – do not dress up your essay with unnecessary padding.

EXERCISE

Write your own checklist on the range of combined skills and personal qualities that you will need to be at your best in an exam.

✓ ....

✓ ....

✓ ....

✓ ....

✓ ....

With reference to the above exercise, skills might include such things as critical thinking, time and task management, focus on issues, and quick identification of problems to address. Personal qualities might include factors such as confidence, endurance, resilience and stress control.

3.7	
tips on interpreting essay and exam questions	

This section will enable you to:

- focus on the issues that are relevant and central
- read questions carefully and take account of all the words
- produce a balanced critique in your outline structures
- screen for the key words that will shape your response
- focus on different shades of meaning between "critique", "evaluate", "discuss" and "compare and contrast"

What Do You See?

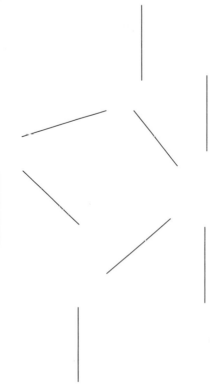

The suggested explanation for visual illusions is the inappropriate use of cues – that is, we try to interpret three-dimensional figures in the real world with the limitations of a two-dimensional screen (the retina in the eye). We use cues such as shade, texture, size, background and so on to interpret distance, motion, shape and so forth, and we sometimes use these inappropriately. Another visual practice we engage in is to "fill in the blanks" or join up the lines (as in the case of the nine lines above – we might assume to be a chair). Our tendency is to impose the nearest similar and familiar template on that which we think we see. The same occurs in the social world – when we are introduced to someone of a different race we may (wrongly) assume certain things about them. The same can also apply to the way you read exam or essay questions. In these cases you are required to "fill in the blanks", but what you fill in may be the wrong interpretation of the question. This is especially likely if you have primed yourself to expect certain questions to appear in an exam, but it can also happen in course work essays.

Although examiners do not deliberately design questions to trick you or trip you up, they cannot always prevent you from seeing things that were not designed to be there. When one student was asked what the four seasons are, the response given was, "salt, pepper, mustard and vinegar". This was not quite what the examiner had in mind!

> *Go into the exam room, or address the course work essay well prepared, but be flexible enough to structure your learned material around the slant of the question.*

A Politician's Answer

Politicians are renowned for refusing to answer questions directly or for evading them through raising other questions. A humorous example is that when a politician was asked, "Is it true that you always answer questions by asking another?", the reply given was, "Who told you that?" Therefore, make sure that you answer the set question, although there may be other questions that arise out of this for further study that you might want to highlight in your conclusion. As a first principle, you must answer the set question and not another question that you had hoped for in the exam or essay.

> *Do not leave the examiner feeling like the person who interviews a politician and goes away with the impression that the important issues have been sidestepped.*

Example: Focus on formulating your answer

Discuss the key factors involved in establishing and maintaining a productive group.

Directly relevant points:

- Social facilitation
- Drive theory
- Evaluation apprehension
- Distraction conflict
- Task taxonomy

Less relevant points:

- Ringlemann effect
- Group size
- Group cohesiveness
- Socialisation

Although some of the points listed in the second column may be relevant to groups overall, they are not as directly relevant as the key thinkers in this area. However, some of the points could be mentioned briefly without going off on a tangent.

> Be ready to resist the wealth of fascinating material at your disposal that is not directly relevant to your question.

Missing Your Question

A student bitterly complained after an exam that the topic he had revised so thoroughly had not been tested in the exam. The first response to that is that students should always cover enough topics to avoid selling themselves short in the exam – the habit of "question spotting" is always a risky game to play. However, the reality in the anecdotal example was that the question the student was looking for was there, but he had not seen it. He had expected the question to be couched in certain words and he could not find these when he scanned over the questions in blind panic. Therefore, the simple lesson is: always read over the questions carefully, slowly and thoughtfully. This practice is time well spent.

> You can miss the question if you restrict yourself to looking for a set form of words and if you do not read over all the words carefully.

Write it Down

If you write down the question you have chosen to address, and perhaps quietly articulate it with your lips, you are more likely to process fully its true meaning and intent. Think of how easy it is to misunderstand a question that had been put to you verbally because you have misinterpreted the tone or emphasis.

> If you read over the question several times, you should be aware of all the key words and will begin to sense the connections between the ideas, and will envisage the possible directions you should take in your response.

Take the following humorous example:

(a)   What is that on the road ahead?
(b)   What is that on the road, a head?

Question (a) calls for the identification of an object (what is that?), but question (b) has converted this into an object that suggests there has been a decapitation! Ensure therefore that you understand the direction the question is pointing you towards so that you do not go off at a tangent. One word in the question that is not properly attended to can throw you completely off track, as in the following example:

(a)   Discuss whether the love of money is the root of all evil.
(b)   Discuss whether money is the root of all evil.

These are two completely different questions, as (a) suggests that the real problem with money is inherent in faulty human use – that is, money itself may not be a bad thing if it is used as a servant and not a master. Whereas (b) may suggest that behind every evil act that has ever been committed, money is likely to have been implicated somewhere in the motive.

Pursue a Critical Approach

In psychology you are expected to write critically rather than merely descriptively, although it may be necessary to use some minimal descriptive substance as the raw material for your debate.

Example: A critical approach

To what extent can prejudice and discrimination be explained by personality factors?

Can be explained by personality factors:

- Authoritarianism – unconscious childhood hostilities are displaced onto minorities.
- Dogmatism – individuals have a rigid cognitive style that leads to intolerance.

Cannot be explained by personality factors:

- Frustration leads to aggression.
- Perception of an outgroup, and therefore social factors, result in prejudice.

Given that the question is about a critical evaluation of the evidence, you would need to address the issues one by one from both standpoints.

Analyse the Parts

In an effective sports team the end product is always greater than the sum of the parts. Similarly, a good essay cannot be constructed without reference to the parts. Furthermore, the parts will arise as you break down the question into the components it suggests to you. Although the breaking down of a question into components is not sufficient for an excellent essay, it is a necessary starting point.

To achieve a good response to an exam or essay question, aim to integrate all the individual issues presented in a manner that gives shape and direction to your efforts.

Example 1

Discuss the view that studies of conformity and obedience demonstrate the process of social influence.

Two parts to this question are clearly suggested – conformity and obedience – and you would need to do justice to each in your answer. Other issues that arise in relation to these are left for you to suggest and discuss. Examples might be types of social influence.

Example 2

Evaluate the advantages and disadvantages of theories of aggression.

This is a straightforward question in that you have two major sections – advantages and disadvantages. You are left with the choice of the issues that you wish to address, and you can arrange these in the order you prefer. Your aim should be to ensure that you do not have a lopsided view, including both support and criticisms of the theories.

> *Give yourself plenty of practice at thinking of questions in this kind of way – both with topics on and not on your course. Topics not on your course that really interest you may be a helpful way to "break you in" to this critical way of thinking.*

Luchins and Learning Sets

In a series of experiments, Luchins allowed children to learn how to solve a problem that involved pouring water from and into a series of jugs of various sizes and shapes. He then gave them other problems that could be solved by following the same sequence. However, when he later gave them another problem that could be solved through a simpler sequence, they went about solving it through the previously learned procedure. In this case the original approach was more difficult, but it had become so set in the children's minds that they were blinded to the shorter, more direct route.

Example: How much did the wealthy Scottish man leave behind?

The story is told of a wealthy Scottish man who died, and no one in his village knew how much he had left behind. The issue was debated and gossiped about for some time, but one man claimed that he knew how much the man had left. He teased all the debaters and gossips in the village night after night. Eventually he let his big secret out, and the answer was that the rich man had left "all of it" behind! No one in the village had been able to work out the mischievous man's little ruse because of the convergent thinking style they used.

Some exam questions may require you to be divergent in the way you think (that is, not just one obvious solution to the problem). This may mean being like a detective in the way you investigate and problem solve. The only difference is that you may need to set up the problem as well as the solution!

Get into the habit of "stepping sideways" and looking at questions from several angles. The best way to do this is by practice, for example, on previous exam papers.

Checklist: Understanding questions fully

- ✓ Read over the chosen question several times.
- ✓ Write it down to ensure that it is clear.
- ✓ Check that you have not omitted any important aspect or point of emphasis.
- ✓ Ensure that you do not wrongly impose preconceived expectations on the question.
- ✓ Break the question into parts (dismantle and rebuild).

EXERCISE

Write your own checklist on any additional points of guidance for exams that you have picked up from tutors or textbooks.

....

....

....

....

....

When Asked to Discuss

Students often ask how much of their own opinion they should include in an essay. In a discussion, when you raise one issue, another one can arise out of it. One tutor used to introduce his lectures by saying that he was going to "unpack" the arguments. When you unpack an object (such as a new desk that has to be assembled), you first remove the overall packaging, such as a large box, and then proceed to remove the covers from all the component parts. After that you attempt to assemble all the parts, according to the given design, so that they hold together in the intended manner. In a discussion your aim should be not just to identify and define all the parts that contribute, but also to show where they fit (or don't fit) into the overall picture.

> *Although the word "discuss" implies some allowance for your opinion, remember that this should be informed opinion rather than groundless speculation. There must also be direction, order, structure and end product.*

Checklist: Features of a response to a "discuss" question

- ✓ Contains a chain of issues that lead into each other in sequence.
- ✓ Clear shape and direction is unfolded in the progression of the argument.
- ✓ Underpinned by reference to findings and certainties.
- ✓ Identification of issues where doubt remains.
- ✓ Tone of argument may be tentative but should not be vague.

If a Critique is Requested

One example that might help clarify what is involved in a critique is the hotly debated topic of the physical punishment of children. It would be important in the interest of balance and fairness to present all sides and shades of the argument. You would then look at whether there is available evidence to support each argument, and you might introduce issues that have been coloured by prejudice, tradition, religion and legislation. It would be an aim to identify emotional arguments, arguments based on intuition and to get down to those arguments that really have solid evidence-based support. Finally, you would want to flag up where the strongest evidence appears to lie, and you should also identify issues that appear to be inconclusive. It would be expected that you should, if possible, arrive at some certainties.

EXERCISE

Write your own summary checklist for the features of a critique. You can either summarise the above points, or use your own points or a mixture of the two.

....

....

....

....

....

If Asked to Compare and Contrast

When asked to compare and contrast, you should be thinking in terms of similarities and differences. You should ask what the two issues share in common, and what features of each are distinct. Your preferred strategy for tackling this might be to work first through all the similarities, then through all the contrasts (or vice versa). Alternatively, you could work through one similarity and contrast, followed by another similarity and contrast and so on.

Example: Write an essay that compares and contrasts theories of the self

1 *Similarities between theories*

  (a) Agreed social and personal identities.
  (b) Consideration of individual centred approach.

2 *Differences between theories*

  (a) Focus on cognitions – self-perception theory.
  (b) Focus on social context – social comparison, self-categorisation.

> When you compare and contrast, you should aim to paint a true picture of the full "landscape".

Whenever Evaluation is Requested

A worked example of evaluation is given below, based on a television soap opera director.

Imagine that you are a television director for a popular soap opera. You have observed in recent months that you have lost some viewers to a soap opera on a rival channel. All is not yet lost because you still have a loyal hard core of viewers who have remained faithful. Your programme has been broadcasted for ten years and there has, until recently, been little change in viewing figures. The rival programme has used some fresh ideas and new actors and has a big novelty appeal. It will take time to see if their level of viewing can be sustained, but you run the risk that you might lose some more viewers at least in the short term. On the other hand, with some imagination you might be able to attract some viewers back. However, there have been some recent murmurings about aspects of the programme being stale, repetitive and predictable. You have been given the task of evaluating the programme to see if you can ascertain why you have retained the faithful but lost other viewers, and what you could do to improve the programme without compromising the aspects that work. In your task you might want to review past features (retrospective), outline present features (perspective) and envisage positive future changes (prospective).

This illustration may provoke you to think about how you might approach a question that asks you to evaluate some theory or concept in your own academic field of study. Some summary points to guide you are presented below:

- Has the theory/concept stood the test of time?
- Is there a supportive evidence base that would not easily be overturned?
- Are there questionable elements that have been or should be challenged?
- Does more recent evidence point to a need for modification?
- Is the theory/concept robust and likely to be around for the foreseeable future?
- Could it be strengthened through being merged with other theories/concepts?

EXERCISE

Write your own checklist on what you remember or understand about each of the following: "Discuss", "Compare and contrast", "Evaluate" and "Critique" (just a key word or two for each). If you find this difficult, then you should read the section again and then try the exercise.

....

....

....

....

It should be noted that the words presented in the above examples might not always be the exact words that will appear on your exam script – for example, you might find "analyse" or "outline" or "investigate" and so on. The best advice is to check over past exam papers and familiarise yourself with the words that are most recurrent.

3.8	
summary	

Part three has been designed to give you reference points to measure where you are at in your studies, and to help you map out the way ahead in manageable increments. It should now be clear that learning should not merely be a mechanical exercise, such as just memorising and reproducing study material. Quality learning also involves making connections between ideas, thinking at a deeper level by attempting to understand your material, and developing a critical approach to learning. However, this cannot be achieved without the discipline of preparation for lectures, seminars and exams, or without learning to structure your material (headings and subheadings) and to set each unit of learning within its overall context in your subject and programme. An important device in learning is to develop the ability to ask questions (whether written, spoken or silent). Another useful device in learning is to illustrate your material and use examples that will help make your study fun, memorable and vivid. It is useful to set problems for yourself that will allow you to think through solutions and therefore enhance the quality of your learning.

On the one hand, there are the necessary disciplined procedures such as preparation before each learning activity and consolidation afterwards. It is also vital to keep your subject materials in organised folders so that you can add/extract/replace materials when you need to. On the other hand, there is the need to develop personality qualities such as feeding your confidence, fuelling your motivation and turning stress responses to your advantage. Part three has presented strategies to guide you through finding the balance between these organised and dynamic aspects of academic life.

Your aim should be to become an "all-round student" who engages in and benefits from all the learning activities available to you (lectures, seminars, tutorials, computing, labs, discussions, library work and so on), and to develop all the academic and personal skills that will put you in the driving seat to academic achievement. It will be motivating and confidence building for you, if you can recognise the value of these qualities, both across your academic programme and beyond graduation to the world of work. They will also serve you well in your continued commitment to lifelong learning.

glossary	

Actor-observer effect – leads to error as attributions about our own behaviour tend to be external and unstable, but for others tend to be internal and stable. This may be because we do actually have different perspectives on behaviour, so perceive other's behaviour as more important and noticeable than our own.

Affection – the basic need for the company of others (humans).

Ageism – this is prejudice and discrimination on the basis of age. Generally the negativity will be expressed towards the older generation, who are perceived to make little contribution to society compared to the young.

Aggregation principle – rather than looking at general measures of attitudes, those taken over time are better at predicting behaviour rather than specific examples as they reflect different situations and times.

Aggression – Berkowitz (1993) saw aggression as any act "involving behaviour, either physical or symbolic, performed with the intention of harming someone".

Altruism – behaviour that is "voluntary, costly to the altruist and motivated by something other than the expectation of material or social reward" (Walster & Piliavin, 1972: 167).

Anchoring and adjustment heuristic – use a starting value on which to base judgements.

Attitude – "a mental state of readiness, organised through experience, exerting a directive or dynamic influence upon the individual's response to all objects and situations with which it is related" (Allport, 1935: 150).

Attitude formation – the formation of attitudes based on experience and emotion.

Attribution – the process of assigning causes of our own behaviour to that of others'.

Attribution theory – Weiner (1986) was interested in the attributions made for experiences of success and failure and believed these were made based on three areas: locus which could be internal or external (see Rotter, 1966); stability, which is whether the cause is stable or changes over time; and controllability.

Authoritarian personality – Adorno found that a certain type of personality – the authoritarian personality – referred to an individual who tended to be hostile, rigid and inflexible, intolerant and someone who therefore upholds traditional values and respects authority that may have originated in childhood. Unconscious hostilities from childhood are simply displaced onto minority groups and their own antisocial views are projected onto minorities, thus serving an ego defensive function.

Availability heuristic – makes judgements about predicted events and behaviour as they are easily available in memory.

Balance theory – Heider (1958) focuses on three elements: a person (P), another person (O) and an attitude, object or topic (X). It is therefore a triad of three elements and a person tries to ensure consistency, or a balance, between these because this is preferable. Altogether there are eight possible combinations of relationships between two people and an object – four balanced and four unbalanced. If there is no such cognitive consistency, then it motivates attitude change.

Behaviour – these interactions can be measured objectively.

Behaviourism – states in which behaviour can be shaped by positive, negative or no reinforcement such that desirable behaviour can be produced and undesirable behaviour discouraged.

Belief congruence theory – there is a resistance to change when encountering contradictory beliefs and a need to retain the existing belief system. In his belief congruence theory, Rokeach (1960) proposed that prejudice derives from dissimilar views amongst people (there is incongruence).

Bystander intervention – intervening behaviour offered by those witnessing an emergency.

Bystander-calculus model – (Piliavin et al., 1969) propose that bystanders will offer help depending on their level of arousal and on the costs and rewards of potential actions. It involves three stages: experiencing physiological arousal; interpreting and labelling that arousal; and evaluating the consequences (rewards/ costs) of offering help.

Case studies – these focus on one individual and their behaviour, thoughts, feelings and experiences.

Category – groups of objects are perceived in a similar way.

Catharsis – release of feelings that have built up (for example, aggression).

Cognitive algebra – (Anderson, 1965, 1978, 1981) impressions of people are formed by combining pieces of information about a person to complete a whole picture. This approach looks at how information that is positive or negative is put together to give a general impression. To do this, three algebraic processes/ models can be used: *summation* – an impression is created by adding together each piece of information about an individual; *averaging* – there is an averaging of the characteristics of a person such that they are seen as more favourable if, on the whole, they display more positive attributes; and *weighted average* – an impression is created by giving weight/value to pieces of information about the person, and this links back to the idea of Asch's central traits (1946) where some characteristics are seen as more important than others.

Cognitive consistency – because inconsistency is uncomfortable people attempt to achieve cognitive consistency.

Cognitive dissonance – if we hold beliefs, attitudes or cognitions that are different, then we experience dissonance – this is an inconsistency that causes discomfort. We are motivated to reduce this by either changing one of our thoughts, beliefs or attitudes or selectively attending to information which supports one of our beliefs and ignores the other (*selective exposure hypothesis*). Dissonance occurs when there are difficult choices or decisions or when people participate in behaviour that is contrary to their attitude. Dissonance is thus brought about by: effort justification (when aiming to reach a modest goal); induced compliance (when people are forced to comply contrary to their attitude); and free choice (when weighing up decisions).

Cognitive model of bystander intervention – (Latane & Darley, 1970) – this model suggests that a bystander makes a series of decisions before deciding whether or not to offer help to a victim. This includes initially noticing an event or that someone needs help, interpreting the situation as an emergency, deciding whether or not to assume responsibility, knowing what to do and then implementing a decision.

Cognitive psychology – sees human beings as information processors but influences social psychology as processes such as memory, attention and perception can be applied to understanding social behaviour.

Collective identity – the self is seen collectively as part of shared views of a group and their actions.

Collective mind – the idea that individuals form a "collective" or group mind derived from social norms/the social context.

Collective self – the self is viewed in terms of collective group membership (of one group against another).

Communication networks – these are networks that provide rules on communications between different roles in the group. Models include those involving three, four or five members with greater performance being achieved on simple tasks when there is more centralisation, but this is less crucial on complex tasks because the complexity of information would overwhelm a single person. To be effective, both a formal and informal communication structure exists in most groups.

Compatibility/correspondence theory – attitudes predict behaviour if there is compatibility/correspondence in terms of the target, context, action and time. Behaviour can be predicted from specific and also general attitudes.

Compliance – although a person may privately maintain their own view, they will publicly display the attitudes or behaviour of the majority because they want to be accepted as part of that group and have a desire to be liked (normative social influence).

Confidentiality – participants must be assured that all information gained during investigations will be kept confidential.

Configuration model – (Asch, 1946) in forming an impression of others we focus on key factors/pieces of information called "central traits", and these are very important in forming a final impression of people. The "halo effect" occurs when one positive attribute leads to perception of others (and the same for negative traits). Less important aspects (peripheral traits) are also involved, but are less significant, in this process.

Conformity/majority social influence – people change their behaviour so that they adopt that of the majority. People are most likely to conform because they have a desire to be liked and a desire to be right (normative and informational social influence) and so publicly (although not necessarily privately) display the attitudes and behaviours of the dominant group.

Contact hypothesis – Allport (1920) proposed that prejudice can be reduced when there is contact between groups, and this can include equal status contact and the pursuit of common (superordinate) goals. Segregation leads to ignorance and reinforcement of negative stereotyping, but prejudice can be reduced by ensuring contact between groups such that they come to realise that there is some equal status and that each group is made up of individuals. If conflicting groups are made to co-operate with each other to achieve a common goal, then this may also reduce prejudice.

Correlation – measures the strength of the relationship between two variables; for example, it tests if there is a relationship between two things. It does not, however, test cause and effect – so it does not say that one thing causes the other, but simply says there is some relationship between two things.

Correspondent inference theory – (Jones & Davis, 1965) people make attributions based on, or corresponding to, underlying traits, drawing on freely chosen behaviour, whether behaviour is common/expected or not, if it is socially desirable, has important consequences or if it is personal or not.

Covariation/ANOVA model – (Kelley, 1973) our knowledge of behaviour is used to make attributions based on the consensus, consistency and distinctiveness of the available information. It looks at how such information co-varies with each other: is there consensus (do other people behave in the same way as the individual), consistency (has the individual behaved in the same way in the past, or on each occasion) or distinctiveness (where different behaviour is shown in similar, but different, circumstances)? According to this model, an internal (person) attribution will be made when there is low consensus and distinctiveness but high consistency, otherwise an external (situational) attribution is made. If consistency is low, causes are discounted and alternatives sought.

Debriefing – whilst debriefing does not justify unethical practices, it is used to further the participants' understanding of the research aims and processes in which they have taken part. This is to ensure that they do not later suffer any psychological harm from their participation and allows them to gain a full understanding of what and why procedures have been used and what results were then obtained.

Deception – according to the BPS ethical guidelines, it is unethical to deceive/mislead/withhold information from participants, knowingly or unknowingly, about the aims or procedures of any research, unless there is strong scientific justification agreed by an ethics committee.

Dehumanisation – people have their dignity taken away, they are seen only as a group member based on shared characteristics and not as individual human beings.

Deindividuation – the individual relinquishes individual responsibility for actions and sees behaviour as a consequence of group norms and expectations.

Dependent variable (DV) – this is what one hopes alters as a result of what is *changed* (so the DV measures any changes the IV has produced).

Desensitisation – explains media violence by claiming that exposure to violence decreases one's usual emotional responsiveness to it. One research study by Sheehan (1983), who studied 5–10-year-olds, identified a correlation between children's exposure to violent television and later real-life aggression, but only in the older children. Consistency of aggressive tendencies, fantasy and parental characteristics also played a role.

Diffusion of responsibility – the less help is offered, the more people present, as responsibility for helping is divided or "diffused" between them because each person assumes someone else will help.

Discrimination – behaviour that reflects prejudice.

Disinhibition – the norms that usually stop us from acting in a particular way are not present, so this makes aggression legitimate.

Dissolution – breakdown of relationships.

Distraction conflict – we can only attend to a limited amount of information and therefore if performing a simple task we can also attend to the demands of the group, but if we try to focus on both types of demands, then arousal increases and performance declines.

Dogmatism/closed-mindedness – Rokeach (1960) argued that dogmatism or closed-mindedness accounts for prejudice because such, individuals have a rigid and intolerant cognitive style that predisposes them to be prejudiced simply because it is a way of thinking.

Drive theory of social facilitation – arousal "drives" social behaviour and increased arousal occurs as a natural instinct in the presence of others. As such, increased arousal due to the audience may increase performance on well-learned/easy tasks, but impair performance when this is not the case.

Ecological validity – research/theories that are valid and applicable in the real world.

Effort justification – cognitive dissonance arises when much effort is applied but only to achieve a modest goal.

Elaboration likelihood model – attitude change occurs as a result of persuasion, but the effect this has depends on the degree of cognitive effort applied to the message. If it requires much effort, a *central route* is used which involves understanding the argument, picking up on the most important points and considering a balanced argument. When the message requires little effort, then a *peripheral route* is used. Personal involvement, accountability and negative mood all increase message elaboration, as do individual differences in the need for cognition (engagement and enjoyment in thinking about problems).

Emotional lability – (Schachter, 1964) – experience of emotion depends on attributions made about those feelings. They involve a physical component which leads to arousal, but also a cognitive component. This relies on the label given, or attribution made, and it is this attribution that will then determine the actual emotion experienced.

Empathic concern – help is offered because it is only by seeing someone else's viewpoint that one "experiences" their feelings and therefore helps.

Empathy – an emotion consistent with someone else's feelings, it is something that allows us to identify with another's emotions.

Empathy arousal hypothesis – according to Batson (1994), one helps others because of empathy, so one identifies with another's distress and is then motivated to help in order to stop this feeling. This process involves perspective taking (seeing someone else's viewpoint), personal distress (feeling emotional) and empathic concern. Help is then offered because it is only by seeing someone else's viewpoint that one "experiences" their feelings and therefore helps.

Equity theory – relationships are based on a fair/equal balance of input/output or rewards and costs by both partners. Adams (1965) predicts that equity exists when A's outcomes divided by A's inputs equals B's outcomes divided by B's inputs. Such equity is guided by the equity norm, social welfare norm (resources are allocated according to need) and the egalitarian norm (everyone should get equal amounts). If there is inequity, then we alter our input or restructure our perceived input so it does not seem so unequal. If this does not work, then the relationship ends.

Ethology – explains behaviour as genetic and evolutionary, aiding the survival and functioning of a species.

Evaluation – requires you to say what is good or bad about a theory/argument/study and focuses on *how* a theory or idea can be supported by research and *how* it can be criticised by research. Your ability to demonstrate this skill will differentiate the class of degree you receive.

Evaluation apprehension – it is not the presence of others that causes arousal, but the apprehension of being evaluated by others. If we are confident of our ability, then being watched/having an audience will increase performance, but if we are not confident and we are worrying about being evaluated, then our arousal increases because of evaluation apprehension and so performance declines.

Evolutionary social psychology – assumes that behaviour is simply the result of biological/innate factors and that social behaviour occurs because it has helped us to adapt, survive and therefore evolve over time.

Excitation-transfer theory – aggression is the result of learning, arousal or excitation from an external stimuli and an individual's interpretation of that arousal.

Aggression is therefore a result of a sequence whereby arousal is generated and then labelled as a specific emotion, which leads to such behaviour.

Expectancy value models – predict that the course of action is determined by expected outcome and value, with individuals choosing the course most likely to lead to positive outcomes. Includes the theory of reasoned action and the theory of planned behaviour.

Expectancy value technique – attitudes towards an object are the result of the "sum of expectancy × the value" products where only relevant features are attended to by the person.

Experimental method – investigates cause and effect, so if one variable is changed (the IV) will it have an effect on the DV/what you are measuring.

Exposure and familiarity – according to Zajonc's "mere exposure effect" (1968), the more exposure and familiarity, the higher the preference, and as proximity leads to exposure it may include familiarity, and this also leads us to feel more comfortable, hence increasing the chances of attraction. Familiarity is rewarding as it leads to participation in joint activities, increases self-esteem, eases communication and leads to reciprocal liking.

External attribution – belief that things occur by chance and are the result of the environment.

False consensus effect – since consensus was an important factor in Kelly's model, its role has been closely examined and it has been discovered that errors occur because we tend to assume that our behaviour is typical, even when this may not be the case, and therefore assume that everyone else would make the same assumptions. This is most likely to occur when we have strong beliefs about something.

Field experiment – the researcher also deliberately manipulates the IV, but does so in the participant's own natural environment.

Filter model – (Kerckhoff & Davis, 1962) the probability of two people meeting is determined by demographic variables/social circumstances. Thus our social group is filtered and we are attracted to those with whom we share similarities. Next, further filtering is based on the sharing of common basic values and then the relationship between emotional needs. This filtering process thus determines the relationship stages.

Free choice – cognitive dissonance arising from inconsistencies when weighing up decisions.

Frustration-aggression hypothesis – frustration always causes aggression and aggression is always the result of frustration. Aggression is therefore triggered by frustrating situations and events. So people are driven to aggression in order to reduce frustration and to thus maintain a balanced internal state. Berkowitz (1963) modified this original hypothesis to suggest that frustration actually produces a state of *readiness* for aggression, but that cues in the situation are also important. This led to the idea of the "weapons effect" whereby aggression is produced more readily if a weapon is present (especially one associated with frustration) rather than a neutral object.

Fundamental attribution error – people tend to blame behaviour on the individual and their characteristics, and see the individual as responsible for their own actions. Thus internal, dispositional attributions are made. This occurs because one likes to feel that the world is controllable, and therefore placing blame on stable personal characteristics is easier than considering changeable ones. Attention also tends to focus on the immediate individual rather than other factors involved in the situation. Focus of emotion, theories of forgetting, cultural, developmental and linguistic factors could all account for this error.

Group-based social identity – the self is based on group membership.

Group cohesiveness – is the factor that binds the group together, giving individuals a sense of membership and group identity.

Group socialisation – involves stages that initiate individuals into the group, through a process of commitment and adjustment to changing roles.

Group structure – how a group is structured.

Guttman's scalogram method (1944) – attitudes are measured by the degree of acceptability of various statements, with a single trait being measured along this continuum of acceptability. It is designed such that agreement with strong items correlates with agreement of weaker ones, and likewise for statements to which a person disagrees. Analysis then reveals an underlying attitude.

Heuristic processing – decision rules are used to make a judgement/form an attitude, so use mental shortcuts/cues available.

Heuristic systematic model – a heuristic is a mental shortcut used in the processing of information. When a person has a personal involvement in a situation and attending is therefore important to them, then input/cognitive processes or analysis occurs (systematic processing). In contrast, when personal involvement is low, individuals instead rely on these mental shortcuts to decide on attitude change. Persuasive messages are often processed in this way, as we have a sufficiency threshold where heuristics are used if they give us enough confidence in the attitude we wish to display. The *bias hypothesis* also predicts that when a message is mixed or ambiguous, then heuristics will be used initially, and this may then lead to biased systematic processing.

Hypotheses – these are testable statements of a relationship between two or more variables which should be a precise, testable statement which predicts that two variables are related in some way, and if you alter one of them this may cause the participant to alter the other.

Identification – when membership of a group is important to a person in the social setting, then they adopt the value of the majority both publicly and privately, although this changes once the particular group is no longer of importance.

Impression management – this is where we try to create a good impression of ourselves. Usually we act deliberately to ensure that we give a favourable impression of ourselves.

Independent variable (IV) – this is the thing that the researcher *deliberately manipulates* and so it is the thing that she purposely changes.

Individual centred approach – the study of social behaviour that emphasises individual experience/behaviour.

Individual psychology – all psychology focuses on the human mind and behaviour, but social psychology is a specific subsection as it looks at how processes occur in the presence of others/within the social context.

Individual self – self based on individual traits.

Individual versus collective self – the individual self has personal and private views and individuals act together and may share an identity. The collective self derives from the group. According to Wundt (1897), the collective self emerges from shared language, customs and so on, and individuals cannot therefore be viewed in isolation. Individuals together therefore form a "group mind".

Individualism – influences the rights, values and experiences of the individual over those of society.

Induced compliance – cognitive dissonance arises when people are forced to comply with a modest goal.

Information integration theory – attitudes are constructed in response to information we have about objects, so attitudes are formed by evaluating and averaging information that is collected and stored about a given object.

Informational social influence – people will yield to the majority social influence because they want to be accepted and therefore feel the need to be right/display the correct answer or behaviour in order to gain such acceptance.

Informed consent – according to the BPS ethical guidelines, all participants are required to give consent to take part in scientific research (or in the case of children or other vulnerable groups, this must be given on their behalf) and this entails informing them of the demands, objectives and possible effects of the study. It is believed that only after gaining such information can a participant make an informed decision concerning their willingness to participate.

Innate – factors that are a result of nature/genes. These are characteristics one is born with.

Instinct – a genetically determined, innate drive/impulse/behaviour.

Inter-attitudinal structure – looks at the relationship between different attitudinal objects. Links to explanations such as balance theory.

Internal attribution – one believes they have control over behaviour.

Internalisation – views of the social group are internalised and the behaviour/attitudes of the majority are consistent both publicly and privately.

Interpersonal attraction – looks at relationships, their beginning, processes, maintenance and dissolution/breakdown.

Intra-attitudinal structure – looks at how the relationship between single attitudinal components and how consistent they are. Fishbein (1996) believes that an attitude towards an object is simply the "sum of expectancy × the value" of products, where only relevant features are attended to by the person. Within this there can also be attitudinal ambivalence where favourable and unfavourable beliefs exist together.

Just world hypothesis – according to Lerner & Miller (1978), people get what they deserve and therefore help will only be offered if one feels this is not the case, such that help is offered to try to remove a perceived injustice.

Laboratory experiment – the researcher deliberately manipulates variables using standardised procedures (the same method each time).

Learning/reinforcement – learning through the process of rewards or punishment or no reinforcement.

Likert scale (1932) – attitudes are indicated by selecting a response ranging from strongly agree (5), agree (4), unsure (3), disagree (2), strongly disagree (1), usually designed such that the statements are divided between representing a positive or negative attitude. This helps control for the acquiescence response set (the tendency blindly to agree or disagree consistently with the statements).

Majority social influence – people change their behaviour so that they adopt that of the majority. People are most likely to conform because they have a desire to be liked and a desire to be right (normative and informational social influence) and so publicly (although not necessarily privately) display the attitudes and behaviours of the dominant group.

Message learning approach – a message that is credible, repeated, induces feelings, focuses on the mode of presentation and tries to change attitudes will be more persuasive.

Methodological approach – a scientific approach using replicable/repeatable methods to test a theory or idea.

Methodological influence – the way in which psychologists' methods of working and their research studies influenced the development and thinking about social psychology.

Minimal group paradigm – when divided into artificial (minimal) groups, prejudice results simply from the awareness that there is an "outgroup" (the other group).

Minority social influence – when a minority presents a consistent argument, they may be able to influence the attitudes and behaviour of the majority.

Mood-as-information hypothesis – individuals base their attitudes on evaluations they make about their mood, so use mood to provide information and evaluation of an object.

Mundane realism – is a term often associated with social influence studies as it reflects the extent to which the studies carried out in the laboratories can be said truly to reflect the processes of conformity and obedience in real life.

Naïve psychology – (Heider, 1946, 1958) people inevitably construct theories about themselves and the world, so are "naïve psychologists". We do this because we like to believe behaviour is motivated and is predictable/controllable. This involves making internal and external attributions, that is, distinguishing between personal and environmental factors.

Normative fit – occurs when typical associations and categorisation of group members fit together to explain behaviour such that the categorisation is psychologically salient.

Normative social influence – people have the desire to be liked by the social group and therefore conform to the behaviour and attitudes displayed by the majority.

Obedience – as part of the socialisation process, obedience is a process whereby people behave as they are told to, usually by a figure they perceive to have some authority over them. It is a public display of behaviour rather than a reflection of private beliefs.

Objective – an individual has not placed their own views, preconceived ideas or prejudices on an argument or data collection. It is "value free".

Observation – looks at the behaviour of participants in various situations and sees "a relatively unconstrained segment of a persons freely chosen behaviour as it occurs" (Coolican, 1990). These can be structured or unstructured, but can be carried out in the participant's natural environment.

Person-based social identity – where personal identity is based on factors internalised from group membership.

Person memory – focuses on a propositional model of memory; the idea is that we store propositions and ideas that are linked by associations, with some of these being stronger than others. This is enhanced by rehearsal. Recall involves the use of these links and more is remembered when there is inconsistent information as this involves more thoughts/the use of more links. Person memory is therefore made up of traits and is organised into a range of socially desirable and competent traits. Behaviour is organised according to goals and appearance is based on observation. Impression can then be organised according to the person or group.

Personal identity – where the self is seen as a result of personal relationships and traits.

Persuasion – the characteristics of the person presenting the message, its content and the characteristics of the receiver influence the persausibility and possibility of attitude change. According to Hovland et al. (1953), three general variables (the communication source, message and audience) are involved in persuasion and there are four steps in the process of attitude change: attention, comprehension, acceptance and retention. A source that has credibility and a message that is repeated, induces feelings not just facts, focuses on mode of presentation and is trying to induce attitude change will inevitably be more persuasive (the message learning approach). Gender, self-esteem and individual differences amongst audience members also have an effect. The dual process models of persuasion detailed above (the elaboration likelihood model and heuristic systematic model) suggest that attitude change results from the mode of information processing used by an individual in relation to a message, this being dependent on processing motivation and ability.

Philosophical influence – the way that ideas and beliefs impact on thinking about social psychology.

Physical attractiveness – we are drawn to people who are physically and psychologically attractive. Stereotypes dictate that we believe that those who look physically attractive are also psychologically attractive/have attractive personalities.

Pluralistic ignorance – other bystanders' behaviour is used as a reference for defining the situation as an emergency, so if one person does define it as an emergency and offers help, then this guides further prosocial behaviour. A decision on intervention is therefore made by using others as a guide.

Prejudice – an attitude (usually negative) displayed towards a particular social group/its members.

Privacy regulation theory (PRT) – (Altman, 1975, 1993) people have different needs for company, which they regulate themselves according to their need for privacy. This can operate between dialectic and optimisation principles, so can vary between times or match desired and actual levels.

Prosocial behaviour – any actions that benefit another regardless of the benefits or self sacrifices of the actor (Wispe, 1972).

Protection of participants from harm – according to the BPS ethical guidelines, during the course of research participants should not be subject to any risk of harm beyond that they would normally expect from their lifestyle. Psychologists must prioritise the safety and physical/psychological wellbeing of their participants above all else.

Prototype – a typical association that leads to a perceived difference between groups. Sometimes these prototypes and categorisation of the average group member fit together (structural fit) and explains behaviour (normative fit), in which case the categorisation used is said to be psychologically salient.

Proximity – physical or geographical closeness may determine the probability of attraction (the "field of availables" – Kerckhoff, 1974). This is important as those who live near are more likely to share beliefs, social class and so on, and also incur familiarity, a further factor in the formation of relationships.

Psychodynamic self – the self can only be discovered by psychoanalysis where repressed thoughts are brought into the open. The self tries to maintain a balance between infantile desires (the id) and moral reasoning (the superego), to achieve a state of balance (ego).

Questionnaires – use various types of questions to make a quick and efficient assessment of people's attitudes and which contains fixed or open-ended questions (or both).

Racism – this is prejudice and discrimination on the basis of ethnicity or race. New racism suggests that negative attitudes and behaviours express themselves more subtly than was previously the case, but nonetheless exist as aversive, symbolic, modern, ambivalent or regressive racism. All of these still represent negative attitudes or behaviours towards a racial outgroup.

Realistic conflict – prejudice arises from conflict between groups, especially in the presence of competition. Sherif's robber's cave experiment (Sherif et al., 1961) showed that groups of unknown boys went through three stages when placed in summer camp: group formation (they divided themselves into two distinct groups); intergroup competition; and conflict reduction. Most critically in terms of research on prejudice, it was found that when a tournament took place there was an apparent conflict of interests as both groups aimed to win, and since this was not possible hostility emerged. Thus prejudice and discrimination could result from such a conflict in the environment.

Reciprocal liking – the reciprocity principle suggests that we like those who like us, and vice versa for those whom we dislike. We are therefore most attracted to those who like us; however, there are individual differences in this and our need to feel secure and our self-esteem needs. This is due to the reward–cost model, that is, we are attracted to those who reciprocate and reward us rather than involving ourselves in personal relationships where there may be personal costs. Alternatively, the gain–loss theory (Aronson & Linder, 1965) may explain this, where we are actually attracted more to people who start off by disliking us before changing their minds, as here we gain liking. In contrast, we dislike those whom initially like us and then change their minds (and hence we lose reciprocal liking).

Relation self – the self is seen in terms of relationships with others.

Relational social identity – the self is defined from interactions with specific others.

Relative deprivation – linked to Dollard et al.'s ideas on frustration-aggression (1939), this claims that relative deprivation accounts for prejudice. That is, people experience relative deprivation either of a fraternalistic nature (comparison between groups) or an egoistic nature (comparison between individuals) and this leads to frustration/ aggression and subsequent prejudice as people feel they are not getting what they are entitled to.

Representiveness heuristic – if an event/behaviour is probable, then this is used to make a social judgement.

Reverse discrimination – discrimination which favours a minority group. This may have short-term benefits.

Ringelmann effect (1913) – individual effort on a task decreases as group size increases, due to co-ordination and motivation loss.

Role of media – in aggression the role of media may be important due to social learning and desensitisation.

Role of norms – according to the norm of reciprocity, aggression may simply result from the fact that someone who is the victim of aggression feels that it is therefore the norm to reciprocate this and therefore behaves in a similar way. If such behaviour is the norm, it is also the case that behaviour is more likely to be labelled as aggressive.

Roles – like norms, roles are patterns of behaviour, but between those within the group. They exist for the benefit of the group and can be formal or informal. People can also be assigned task or socio-emotional orientated roles. Roles emerge to ensure that there is a division of labour, to set goals and advice on relationships between members and to give them a place within the group.

Scapegoating – Dollard et al. (1939) proposed that frustration always leads to aggression and that aggression is always caused by frustration. When frustration cannot therefore be directly expressed, then it is displaced indirectly onto others (hence one finds a scapegoat!). In this way, prejudice is cathartic as it allows the release of emotional energy.

Schema – a building block of knowledge about a concept, including its attributes.

Scientific – because behaviour can be observed, hypotheses about the possible interaction between factors can be tested and the results/data can be collected and analysed, which gives this area of psychology credibility.

Selective exposure hypothesis – selectively attending to information which supports one of our beliefs but ignores others.

Self-awareness – "a state where you are aware of yourself" (Duval & Wicklund, 1972).

Self-categorisation theory – (Turner, Hogg, Oakes, Reicher & Wetherall, 1987) knowledge of the self may be derived from group membership, which produces a sense of social identity. Group membership encourages behaviour to be attributed to the self and "ingroup".

Self-disclosure – attraction depends on self-disclosure/sharing of intimate feelings with another person; this is therefore important in developing and maintaining relationships, as we tend to disclose information to those we like and those who disclose information to us.

Self-enhancing triad – is where people overestimate their good points and their control of events and are unrealistically optimistic.

Self-esteem – is based on the feelings one has about themselves and the evaluations they make. It is closely linked to social identity as identification with a group, and its societal connotations impacts on self-concept.

Self-fulfilling prophecy – prejudicial expectations influence social interaction such that the behaviour of others may be changed so that it conforms to that set expectation. Thus the self fulfils the prophecy or expectation.

Self-maintenance model – (Tesser, 1988) since making upward social comparisons can decrease self-concept (not feeling good enough), then people may try to ignore their similarity to another person or withdraw from a relationship to maintain a positive self-evaluation.

Self motives – motives which are important because they aid self-knowledge, including validity, consistency and favourability.

Self-perception theory – (Bem, 1967, 1972) this proposes that we derive knowledge about the self from the attributions we make about our own behaviour. It can also be derived from imagining ourselves behaving in a given way. This concept of the self is important in motivating behaviour because performance will be impaired if there is an obviously external cause for it, otherwise an over-justification effect occurs whereby motivation increases as behaviour is, instead, seen as a result of internal factors such as commitment.

Self presentation – impression management can be used to ensure that one creates a good impression.

Self-serving bias – errors are made to ensure that our self-esteem is protected and therefore in order to "serve ourselves" a bias operates whereby we take credit for our successes (so view them internally), but not for failure (so see failure as due to external factors). In part this maintains a sense of control and also a belief in a just world.

Semantic differential scale – (Osgood et al., 1957) this method asks respondents to indicate their response from a list of opposite word pairs (good/bad), and this semantic differential (the difference between meaning) is then used to assess attitude.

Sexism – this is prejudice and discrimination on the basis of a person's gender. Usually this focuses on discrimination against women.

Similarity – attraction occurs because of the similarity of looks, beliefs, attitudes and values. The matching hypothesis is related to similarity as it suggests that people are most likely to show romantic investment if they are matched in their ability to reward each other, including a basis of physical attraction and similarity. People may also become more similar over time.

Similarity heuristic – if events/behaviour can be imagined, then it forms a social judgement as already "simulated".

Social affiliation model – people need to regulate their social contact to achieve a balance (like homeostasis).

Social cognition – looks at the reciprocal interaction between the social world and mental/cognitive processes.

Social cohesion/interpersonal interdependence model – (Hogg, 1993) according to this model, cohesiveness occurs because individuals cannot achieve a goal alone so get together with others such that there is already some interdependence and co-operative interaction. This leads them all to feel goal satisfaction and a mutual sense of reward with interpersonal attraction.

Social comparison theory – (Festinger, 1954) the self is derived from social comparisons where our feelings, thoughts and behaviours are compared to (often similar) others such that a social identity and sense of self emerges.

Social compensation – sometimes when we believe that others will decrease their efforts in a group, we compensate for this by working harder. It is therefore possible that groups work collectively harder than the sum of its individuals.

Social encoding – the social world is processed by the individual and involves: preattentive analysis (the unconscious taking in of information); focusing of attention (considering the identification and categorising of information); comprehension (give it a meaning); and elaborative reasoning (the linking together and elaboration of information). Information may be better socially encoded when it is vivid (information that is emotionally interesting, provokes images and is environmentally close and therefore more salient) and more accessible or easily recalled (primed).

Social exchange theory – relationships are simply social exchange, which depends on profits gained, thus are based on behaviourist principles. There is a cost–reward ratio involved, for example, a calculation of what costs are involved in receiving rewards from others, therefore social exchanges form the basis of relationships for the benefits they provide relative to the input required as a joint process by both parties, with the aim of averaging mutual benefit/profits with minimal costs (minimax strategy). This will be judged partly by using a comparison level/standard for assessing profitability. Attraction is most likely to occur if an exchange is seen to be a positive.

Social facilitation – (Allport, 1924) the presence of others (the social group) can facilitate certain behaviour. It was found that an audience would improve an actor's performance in well-learned/easy tasks, but lead to a decrease in performance on newly learned/difficult tasks due to social inhibition.

Social identity – the self is seen in terms of group membership.

Social identity approach – looks at the relationship between the self and group membership.

Social identity theory – states that individuals need to maintain a positive sense of personal and social identity and this is partly achieved by emphasising the desirability of one's own group, focusing on distinctions between other "lesser" groups. Prejudice occurs directly as a result.

Social impact – the fact that we are part of a social group impacts on our behaviour and attitudes. Group size is especially influential, with our sense of responsibility more diffused the greater the group size.

Social inference – we use social assumptions to make judgements and form impressions of others. This can involve two processes: top-down, which generally rely on schemas and stereotype, and bottom-up, which focuses on specific events and information.

Social influence – is where people are influenced by others such that they try to display the attitude or behaviour of the social group either by obeying or conforming to the majority or the minority. Social influence occurs because of the desire to be liked and the desire to be right (normative and informational social influence).

Social information processing – both the situation and cognitive processes explain aggression because norms and schemas (a building block of existing knowledge) mean that information about the situation is processed and decisions made. This typically involves perceiving cues in the situation, interpreting them, examining one's own goals and responses and behaving appropriately. If a cue appears and is interpreted as aggressive, this information will be processed and produce subsequent aggressive responses.

Social interactionalist theory of coercive action – aggression is the result of trying to achieve social power to either control others, restore justice or assert/protect identities. This may involve harm or injury.

Social learning theory of aggression – aggression is simply the result of rein-forcement, observation and imitation where aggressive behaviour is therefore acquired through direct, or indirect, modelling. Previous experiences of aggres-sion and the likelihood of it being rewarded or punished are key factors in deter-mining whether or not it is displayed and maintained.

Social loafing – is where individual effort decreases (therefore one loafes!) when working in a group rather than alone, or with another. This is related to the free rider effect, where the member takes advantage of the benefits of being part of a group and exploits this without making any meaningful contribution.

Social norms – look at how individuals behave according to the rules of society.

Social psychology – the scientific field that seeks to understand the nature and causes of individual behaviour in social situations.

Social representations – the belief systems that simplify the social world by intro-ducing a shared social reality, guiding social action.

Socio-centred approach – the study of behaviour that emphasises the function and structure of the social context.

Sociocognitive model of attitudes – focuses on the idea of a single component and looks specifically at the evaluation given to an object which they believe is represented by a label, evaluative summary and knowledge structure.

Sociology – differs from social psychology because it focuses on how groups behave – for example, females, juveniles – and emphasises actions of a collec-tive group rather than looking at the individual psychology of the people who make up that group.

Sociometry – (Moreno, 1953) interpersonal attitudes are assessed whereby group members indicate a preferred partner for an activity, and this is used to chart these interrelationships.

Status – a commonly agreed view that is held concerning the value that certain roles, occupants of that role, or indeed whole groups may have. Higher status roles tend to be viewed commonly as valuable and are ones that encourage ini-tiation of ideas that are then adopted by the whole group. Status hierarchies do, however, vary between contexts and times, although some are institutionalised. Status can derive from *specific status characteristics* that relate directly to ability to perform the group task, and *diffuse status characteristics* that are more focused on the values they hold within society.

Stereotype threat – we feel threatened by the fact that we think we will be treated stereotypically and judged according to negative stereotypes, and as a result behave accordingly.

Stereotypes – are used to categorise people, are slow to change, are acquired at an early age, evident in situations of conflict and help make sense of the world.

Stigma – individuals are seen only in terms of some negative characteristic (within the social context) that they are believed to posses. These may be visible such as race or "controllable" such as smoking.

Stimulus-value-role model – (Murstein, 1976, 1986, 1987) initially attraction is based on a stimulus stage (external attraction/factors), then on the similarity of values and finally a role stage based on the successful performance of relationship roles.

Structural fit – occurs when typical associations and categorisation of the average group member fit together.

Symbolic interactionalist self – self emerges as a result of social interaction and the shared meanings and methods of communication (verbal and non-verbal) that result from this. According to Mead's "looking glass self" (1934), our own concept of the self is also derived from seeing ourselves as others see us. Therefore the self emerges as a reflection of society.

Task taxonomy – in deciding whether a group performs better than an individual, there is a need to classify the task according to whether it is divisible or unitary, maximising or optimising, an additive task, a disjunctive task or conjunctive.

Theory of group cohesiveness – (Festinger et al., 1950) proposes that attraction to a group and its members, along with the social interaction and interdependence provided by trying to achieve goals, leads an individual to feel a sense of cohesion towards a group. This feeling of cohesiveness then encourages continuity of membership towards that group and the following of the required norms.

Theory of planned behaviour – emphasises the role of violation and suggested that predictable behaviour is easier if people believe they have control.

Theory of reasoned action – the key factor linking attitudes and behaviour is the predictability of behaviour by intention. This involves subjective norms (perception of others' beliefs), attitudes towards the behaviour, intention and actual behaviour. Behaviour will result if an attitude and social norms are favourable and perceived behaviour control is increased.

Three-factor theory of love – variables that underlie love include: a culture that acknowledges the concept of love; a love object; and emotional arousal.

Thurstone's equal appearing interval scale (1928) – 100 statements assessing extreme negative to positive attitude towards an object are collated and then evaluated, by judges, on an equal interval, 11-point scale until there are 22 statements (11 positive, 11 negative). The average position of each statement is then taken and the statements given to participants who select those with which they agree. Their attitude is then measured by taking an average score of these responses.

Tokenism – a small effort is made to give the impression that help is being offered to the minority group in order to avoid accusations of prejudice/discrimination.

Volkerpsychologie – an area of psychology that looked at the collective mind and emphasised the notion that personality develops because of cultural and community influences, especially through language which is both a social product of the community and a means of particular social thought in the individual.

Weapons effect – there is an increase in violence following the presence of weapons. In a study by Berkowitz & LePage (1967), it was found that the number of electric shocks given to a confederate was greater when the student had themselves received shocks in the presence of nearby guns, thus precipitating violent schemas and increasing the incident of subsequent aggression.

Withdrawal – according to the BPS ethical guidelines, before commencing any research the investigator must assure participants that they may leave the study at any time should they wish to do so, and there is a duty to ensure that the environment permits this. Withdrawal is permitted even if participants have of group norms and expectations.

references

Abrams, D., & Hogg, M. A. (1999). *Social identity and social cognition*. Oxford: Blackwell.

Adams, J. (1965). Inequity in social exchange. In Hogg, M. A., & Vaughan, G. M. (2005). *Social psychology* (4th ed.) (pp. 514–516). London: Pearson Education.

Adams, J. M., & Jones. W. H. (1997). The conceptualisation of material commitment: An integrative analysis. *Journal of Social and Personal Relationships, 11*, 1177–1196.

Adorno, T. W., Frenkel-Brunswick, E., Levinson, D. J., & Sanford, R. M. (1950). *The authoritarian perspective*. New York: Harper.

Ajzen, I. (1988). *Attitudes, personality and behaviour*. Milton Keynes: Open University Press.

Ajzen, I., & Fishbein, M. (1980). *Understanding attitudes and predicting social behaviour*. Englewood Cliffs, NJ: Prentice-Hall.

Allport, F. H. (1920). The influence of the group upon association and thought. *Journal of Experimental Psychology, 3*, 159–182.

Allport, F. H. (1924). *Social psychology*. Boston, MA: Houghton Mifflin.

Allport, G. W. (1935). Attitudes. In Hogg, M. A., & Vaughan, G. M. (2005). *Social psychology* (4th ed.) (p. 150). London: Pearson Education.

Allport, G. W. (1954a). *The nature of prejudice*. Reading, MA: Addison-Wesley.

Allport, G. W. (1954b). *The nature of prejudice,* Reading, MA: Addison-Wesley.

Altemeyer, B. (1988). *Enemies of freedom: Understanding right-wing authoritarianism*. San Francisco: Jossey-Bass.

Altman, I. (1975). *The environment & social behaviour*. Monterey, CA: Brooks.

Altman, I. (1993). Dialectics, physical environment & personal relationships. *Communication Monographs, 60*, 26–34.

Anderson, N. H. (1965). Adding versus averaging as a stimulus combination rule in impression formation. *Journal of Experimental Psychology, 70*, 394–400.

Anderson, N. H. (1978). Cognitive algebra: Integration theory applied to social attitude. In Hogg, M. A., & Vaughan, G. M. (2005). *Social psychology* (4th ed.) (p. 47). London: Pearson Education.

Anderson, N. H. (1981). *Foundation of information integration theory*. New York: Academic Press.

Aristotle (1941). In *Introduction to social psychology* (3rd ed.). Hewstone, M., & Stroebe, W. (2001). (p. 5). Oxford: Blackwell.

Aronson, E., & Linder, D. (1965). Gain and loss of esteem as determinants of interpersonal attractiveness. *Journal of Experimental Social Psychology, 1*, 156–171.

Asch, S. (1956). Studies of independence and conformity: a minimum of one against a unanimous majority. *Psychological Monographs, 70*, 1–70 (whole no. 416).

Asch, S. E. (1946). Forming impressions of personality. *Journal of Abnormal & Social Psychology, 41*, 258–290.

Bandura, A., Ross, D., & Ross, S. A. (1963). Imitation of film-mediated aggressive models. *Journal of Abnormal and Social Psychology, 66*, 3–11.

Baron, A. (1986). Distraction conflict. In Hogg, M. A., & Vaughan, G. M. (2005). *Social psychology* (4th ed.) (p. 281). London: Pearson Education.

Baron, R. A., & Byrne, D. (1991). *Social psychology* (6th ed.). Boston: Allyn and Bacon.

Baron, R. A., Byrne, D., & Suls, J. (1989). *Exploring social psychology* (3rd ed.). Allyn & Bacon.

Baron, R. A., & Richardson, D. R. (1994). *Human aggression.* New York: Plenum.

Baron S., Kerr, N. L., & Miller, N. (1992). *Group processes, group decisions, group action.* Buckingham: Open University Press.

Batson, C. D. (1991). *The altruism question. Toward a social-psychological answer.* Hillsdale, NJ: Lawrence Erlbaum.

Batson, C. D. (1994). Why act for the public good? 4 answers. *Personality & Social Psychology Bulletin, 20*, 603–610.

Baumeister, R. F. (ed.) (1999). *The self in social psychology.* Philadelphia, PA: Psychology Press.

Bem, D. J. (1967). Self-perception. An alternative interpretation of cognitive dissonance. *Psychological Review, 74*, 183–200.

Bem, D. J. (1972). Self-perception theory. In Hogg, M. A., & Vaughan, G. M. (2005). *Social psychology* (4th ed.) (p. 122). London: Pearson Education.

Berkowitz, L. (1993). *Aggression: Its causes & consequences and control.* Philadelphia: PA: Temple University Press.

Berkowitz, L., & LePage, A. (1967). Weapons as aggression-eliciting stimuli. *Journal of Personality and Social Psychology, 7*, 202–207.

Berschield, E., & Walster, E. H. (1978). *Interpersonal attraction* (2nd ed.). Reading, MA: Addison-Wesley.

Brewer, M. B. (2001). The many faces of social identity: Implications for political psychology. *Political Psychology, 22*, 115–125.

Brewer, M. B., & Gardner, W. (1996). Who is this 'we'? Levels of collective identity and self representation. *Journal of Personality & Social Psychology, 71*, 83–93.

Brown, R. (1995). *Prejudice: Its social psychology.* Oxford: Blackwell.

Brown, R. J. (2000). *Group Processes: An Introduction to Group Processes* (2nd ed.). Oxford: Blackwell.

Byrne, D., & Clore, G. L. (1970). A reinforcement model of evaluative responses. *Personality: An International Journal, 1*, 103–128.

Campbell, J. D. (1990). Self-esteem and clarity of the self-concept. *Journal of Personality and Social Psychology, 59*, 538–549.

Carver, C. S., & Scheier, M. F. (1981). *Attitudes and self-regulation: A control theory approach to human behaviour.* New York: Springer.

Chaiken, S. (1980). Heuristic versus systematic processing and the use of source versus message cues in persuasion. *Journal of Personality and Social Psychology, 39,* 752–766.

Comstock, G., & Paik, H. H. (1991). *Television and the American child.* San Diego, CA: Academic Press.

Coolican, H. (1990). *Research methods and statistics in psychology* (2nd ed.). London: Hodder and Stoughton.

Cottrell, N. B. (1972). Social facilitation. In Hogg, M. A. & Vaughan, G. M. (2005). *Social psychology* (4th ed.) (p. 280). London: Pearson Education.

Darley, J. M., & Latane, B. (1968). Bystander intervention in emergencies. Diffusion of responsibility. *Journal of Personality and Social Psychology, 8,* 377–383.

Darwin, C. (1872). *The expression of emotions in man and animals.* Chicago: University of Chicago Press.

Diener, E., Fraser, S. C., Bearman, A. C., & Kelem, R. T. (1976). Effects of deindividuated variables on stealing by Halloween trick-or-treaters. *Journal of Personality and Social Psychology, 33,* 178–183.

Dollard, J., Doob, L. W., Miller, N. E., Mowrer, O. H., & Sears, R. R. (1939). *Frustration & aggression.* New Haven, CT: Yale University Press.

Duck, S. (1992). *Personal relationships, 4: Dissolving personal relationships.* London: Academic Press.

Duval, S., & Wicklund, R. A. (1972). *A theory of objective self-awareness.* New York: Academic Press.

Eagly, A. H., & Chaiken, S. (1993). *The psychology of attitudes.* San Diego, CA: Harcourt Brace Jovanovich.

Festinger, L. (1954). A theory of social comparison processes. *Human Relations, 7,* 117–140.

Festinger, L. (1957). *A theory of cognitive dissonance.* Stanford, CA: Stanford University Press.

Festinger, L. (1964). *Conflict, decisions and dissonance.* Stanford, CA: Stanford University Press.

Festinger, L., & Carlsmith, J. M. (1959). Cognitive consequences of forced compliance. *Journal of Abnormal & Social Psychology, 58,* 203–210.

Festinger, L., Schachter, S., & Back, K. (1950). *Social pressures in informal groups: A study of human factors in housing.* New York: Harper.

Fishbein, M. (1996). A behaviour theory approach to the relations between beliefs about an object and the attitude toward the object. In Hewstone, M., & Stroebe, W. (2001). *Introduction to social psychology* (3rd ed.) (pp. 244–245). Oxford: Blackwell.

Fishbein, M., & Ajzen, I. (1974). Attitudes towards objects as predictors of single and multiple behaviour criteria. *Psychological Review, 81,* 59–74.

Fiske, S. T., & Taylor, S. E. (1991). *Social cognition* (2nd ed.). New York: McGraw-Hill.

Freud, S. (1920/1984). *Beyond the pleasure principle*. Pelican Freud Library (II). Harmondsworth: Penguin.

Freud, S. (1923/1984). *The ego and the id*. Pelican Freud Library (II). Harmondsworth: Penguin.

Geen, R. G. (1991). Social motivation. *Annual Review of Psychology, 42*, 377–399.

Gunter, B., & McAleer, J. (1997). *Children and television*. London: Routledge.

Guttman, L. A. (1944). A basis for scaling qualitative data. *American Sociological Review, 9*, 139–150.

Haney, C., Banks, C., & Zimbardo, P. (1973a). A study of prisoners and guards in a simulated prison. In Gross, R. D. (1994). *Key studies in psychology* (p. 98). London: Hodder & Stoughton.

Haney, C., Banks, C., & Zimbardo, P. (1973b). Interpersonal dynamics in a simulated prison. *International Journal of Criminology and Penology, 1*, 69–97.

Hatfield, E., & Walster, G. W. (1981). *A new look at love*. Reading, MA: Addison-Wesley.

Hegel (1770–1831). In Hewstone, M., & Stroebe, W. (2001). *Introduction to social psychology* (3rd ed.) (p. 5). Oxford: Blackwell.

Heider, F. (1946). Attribution and cognitive organisation. *Journal of Psychology, 21*, 107–112.

Heider, F. (1958). *Psychology of interpersonal relationships*. New York: Wiley.

Higgins, E. T. (1987). Self-discrepancy: A theory relating self and affect. *Psychological Review, 94*, 319–340.

Hogg, M. A. (1993). Group cohesiveness: A critical review and some new directions. *European review of social psychology, 4*, 85–111.

Hogg, M. A., & Vaughan, G. M. (2005). *Social psychology* (4th ed.). London: Pearson Education.

Hovland, C. I., Janis, I. L., & Kelley, H. H. (1953). *Communication & persuasion*. New Haven, CT: Yale University Press.

Johnson, D. W., & Johnson, F. P. (1987). *Joining together: Group theory and group skills* (3rd ed.). Englewood Cliffs, NJ: Prentice Hall.

Johnson, M. P. (1991). Commitment to personal relationships. In Hogg, M. A., & Vaughan, G. M. (2005). *Social psychology* (4th ed.) (p. 528). London: Pearson Education.

Jones, E. E., & Davis, K. E. (1965). From acts to dispositions: The attribution process in person perception. In Hogg, M. A., & Vaughan, G. M. (2005). *Social psychology* (4th ed.) (pp. 84–5). London: Pearson Education.

Jones, E. E., & Pittman, T. S. (1982). In Hogg, M. A., & Vaughan, G. M. (2005). *Social psychology* (4th ed.) (p. 139). London: Pearson Education.

Katz, D. (1960). The functional approach to the study of attitudes. *Public Opinion Quarterly, 24*, 163–204.

Kelley, H. H. (1950). Warm–cold variables in first impressions of people. *Journal of Personality, 18*, 431–439.

Kelley, H. H. (1967). Attribution in social psychology. In Hogg, M. A., & Vaughan, G. M. (2005). *Social psychology* (4th ed.) (p. 85). London: Pearson Education.

Kelley, H. H. (1972). Causal schemata in the attribution process. In Hogg, M. A., & Vaughan, G. M. (2005). *Social psychology* (4th ed.) (p. 87). London: Pearson Education.

Kelley, H. H. (1973). The process of causal attribution. *American Psychologist, 28*, 107–128.

Kerckhoff, A. C. (1974). The social context of interpersonal attraction. In Gross R. D. (2001). *Psychology: The science of mind and behaviour* (4th ed.) (p. 405). Hodder and Stoughton.

Kerckhoff, A. C. & Davis, K. E. (1962). Value consensus and need complementarity in mate selection. *American Sociology Review, 27*, 295–303.

Klineberg, O. (1940). *Social psychology.* New York: Holt.

Latane, B., & Darley, J. M. (1970). *The unresponsive bystander: why doesn't he help?* New York: Appleton-Century-Crofts.

Latane, B., & Rodin, J. (1969). A lady in distress: Inhibition effects of friends and strangers on bystander intervention. *Journal of Experimental Social Psychology, 5*, 189–202.

Latane, B., Williams, K., & Harkins, S. (1979). Many hands make light work: The causes and consequences of social loafing. *Journal of Personality and Social Psychology, 37*, 822–832.

Lazarus, M., & Steinthal, H. (1860). In Hewstone, M., & Stroebe, W. (2001). *Introduction to social psychology* (3rd ed.) (p. 9). Oxford: Blackwell.

Lee, L. (1984). Sequences in separation: A framework for investigating endings of the personal (romantic) relationship. *Journal of Social and Personal Relationships, 1*, 49–74.

Lerner, M. J., & Miller, D. T. (1978). Just world research and the attribution process: Looking back and ahead. *Psychological Bulletin, 85*, 1030–1051.

Levinger, G. (1980). Toward the analysis of close relationships. In Hogg, M. A., & Vaughan, G. M. (2005). *Social psychology* (4th ed.) (p. 529). London: Pearson Education.

Lewin, K., Lippitt, R., & White, R. K. (1939). Patterns of aggressive behaviour in experimentally created 'social climates'. *Journal of Social Psychology, 10*, 271–299.

Likert, R. (1932). A technique for the measurement of attitudes. *Archives of Psychology, 22* (14), 44–53.

Lorenz, K. (1966). *On aggression.* New York: Harcourt, Brace & Wolard.

Markus, H., & Kityama, S. (1991). Culture and the self: Implications for cognition, emotion and motivation. *Psychological Review, 98*, 224–253.

McDougall, W. (1908). *An introduction to social psychology.* London: Methuen.

McIlroy, D. (2003). *Studying at university: How to be a successful student.* London: Sage.

Mead, G. H. (1934). *Mind, self and society.* Chicago, MA: University of Chicago Press.

Milgram, S. (1963). Behavioural study of obedience. In Gross, R. D. (1994). *Key studies in psychology* (p. 81). London: Hodder & Stoughton.

Milgram, S. (1974). *Obedience to authority.* New York: Harper & Row.

Miller, D. T. (1977). Altruism & the threat to a belief in a just world. *Journal of Experimental Social Psychology, 13* (1), 13–24.

Moreland, R. L., & Levine, J. M. (1982). Socialisation in small groups: Temporal changes in individual-group relations. In Hogg, M. A., & Vaughan, G. M. (2005). *Social Psychology* (4th ed.) (pp. 296–297). London: Pearson Education.

Moreland, R. L. & Levine, J. M. (1984). Role transitions in small groups. In Hogg, M. A., & Vaughan, G. M. (2005). *Social psychology* (4th ed.) (pp. 296–297). London: Pearson Education.

Moreno, J. J. (1953). *Who shall survive?* (2nd ed.). New York: Beacon.

Moscovici, S., Lage, E., & Naffrenchoux, M. (1969). Influence of a consistent minority on the responses of a majority in a colour perception task. *Sociometry, 32*, 365–380.

Murchinson, C. (1935). *Handbook of social psychology.* Worcester, MA: Clark University Press.

Murphy, G. P., & Murphy, L. B. (1931/1937). *Experimental social psychology.* New York: Harper.

Murstein, B. J. (1976). The stimulus-value-role theory of maintenance. In Gross, R. D. (2001). *Psychology: The science of mind and behaviour* (4th ed.). London: Hodder & Stoughton.

Murstein, B. J. (1986). *Paths to marriage.* Beverley Hills, CA: Sage.

Murstein, B. J. (1987). A clarification x extension of the SVR theory of dyadic parting. *Journal of Marriage and the Family, 79*, 929–933.

Osgood, C. E., Suci, G. J., & Tannenbaum, P. H. (1957). *The measurement of meaning.* Urbana, IL: University of Illinois Press.

Paludi, M. A. (1992). *The psychology of women.* Dubuque, IA: Brown.

Petty, R. E., & Cacioppo, J. T. (1986). The elaboration likelihood model of persuasion. In Hogg, M. A., & Vaughan, G. M. (2005). *Social psychology* (4th ed.) (pp. 213–214). London: Pearson Education.

Piliavin, J. A., Piliavin, I. M., Dovido, J., Gaertner, S. L., & Clark, R. D. III. (1981). *Emergency intervention.* New York: Academic Press.

Piliavin, I. M., Rodin, J., & Piliavin, J. A. (1969). Good Samaritanism: An underground phenomenon? *Journal of Personality & Social Psychology, 13*, 289–299.

Ringelmann, M. (1913). In Hogg, M. A., & Vaughan, G. M. (2005). *Social psychology* (4th ed.) (p. 286). London: Pearson Education.

Rokeach, M. (1960). *The open and closed mind.* New York: Basic Books.

Rothbart, M. (1981). In Hogg, M. A., & Vaughan, G. M. (2005). *Social psychology* (4th ed.) (p. 60). London: Pearson Education.

Rotter, J. B. (1966). Generalised expectancies for internal versus external control of reinforcement. *Psychological Monographs, 80*, whole no. 609.

Rubin, Z. (1973). *Liking & loving: An investigation in social psychology.* New York: Holt, Rinehart & Winston.

Schachter, S. (1964). The integration of cognitive and physiological determinants of emotional state. In Hogg, M. A., & Vaughan, G. M. (2005). *Social psychology* (4th ed.) (p. 88). London: Pearson Education.

Schachter, s. & Singer, J. E. (1962). Cognitive, social and physiological determinants of emotional state. *Psychological Review, 69,* 379–399.

Schroeder, D. A., Penner, L. A., Dovidio, J. F., & Piliavin, J. A. (1995). *The psychology of helping and altruism.* New York: McGraw-Hill.

Schwarz, N. (1990). Findings as information. Informational and motivational factors of affective states. In Hewstone, M., & Stroebe, W. (2001). *Introduction to social psychology* (3rd ed.). Oxford: Blackwell.

Sedikides, C. (1993). Assessment, enhancement and verification determinants of the self-evaluation process. *Journal of Personality and Social Psychology, 65,* 317–338.

Sedikides, C., & Gregg, A. P. (2003). Portraits of the self. In Hogg, M. A., & Vaughan, G. M. (2005). *Social psychology* (4th ed.) (p. 118). London: Pearson Education.

Sheehan, P. W. (1983). Age trends and the correlates of children's television viewing. *Australian Journal of Psychology, 35,* 417–431.

Sherif, M. (1935a). A study of some social factors in perception. *Archives of Psychology, 27,* 1–60.

Sherif, M. (1935b). *The psychology of social norms.* New York: Harper and Row.

Sherif, M., Harvey, O. J., White, B. J., Hood, W., & Sherif, C. (1961). *Intergroup conflict and cooperation, the robbers cave experiment.* Norman, OK. University of Oklahoma Institute of Intergroup Relations.

Steele, C. M. (1988). The psychology of self–affirmation: Sustaining the integrity of the self. In Berkowitz, L. (ed). *Advances in experimental social psychology.* Vol. 21 (pp. 261–302). New York: Academic Press.

Steiner, I. D. (1972). *Group processes and productivity.* New York: Academic Press.

Sternberg, R. J. (1988). *A triangle of love.* New York: Basic Books.

Tajfel, H. (1957). Value and the perceived judgement of magnitude. *Psychological Review, 64,* 192–204.

Tajfel, H. (1959). Quantitative judgment in social perception. *British Journal of Psychology, 50,* 16–29.

Tajfel, H. (1974). Social identity and intergroup behaviour. *Social Science Information, 13,* 65–93.

Tajfel, H., Billig, M., Bundy, R. P., & Flament, C. (1971). Social categorisation and intergroup behaviour. *European Journal of Social Psychology, 1,* 149–177.

Tajfel, H., & Turner, J.C. (1979). An integrative theory of intergroup conflict. In Hogg, M. A., & Vaughan, G. M. (2005). *Social psychology* (4th ed.) (pp. 127–130). London: Pearson Education.

Taylor, S. E., & Brown, J. D. (1988). Illusion and well-being: A social psychological perspective on mental health. *Psychological Bulletin, 103,* 193–210.

Tesser, A. (1988). Toward a self-evaluation maintenance model of social behaviour. In Hogg, M. A., & Vaughan, G. M. (2005). *Social psychology* (4th ed.) (p. 124). London: Pearson Education.

Thurstone, L. L. (1928). Attitudes can be measured. *American Journal of Sociology, 83,* 529–554.

Triplett, N. (1898). The dynamogenic factors in pacemaking and competition. *American Journal of Psychology, 9*, 507–533.

Tuckman, B. W. (1965). Developmental sequences in small groups. *Psychological Bulletin, 63*, 384–399.

Turner, J. C. (1975). Social comparison and social identity: some prospects for intergroup behaviour. *European Journal of Social Psychology, 5*, 5–34.

Turner, J. C., Hogg, M. A., Oakes, P. J., & Reicher, S. D. (1987). *Rediscovering the social group: A self-categorisation theory.* Oxford: Blackwell.

Walster, E., & Piliavin, J. A. (1972). Equity and the innocent bystander. *Journal of Social Issues, 28* (3), 165–189.

Weary, G., Stanley, M. A., & Harvey, J. H. (1989). *Attribution.* New York: Springer-Verlag.

Weiner, B. (1986). *An attribution theory of motivation and emotion.* New York: Springer.

Winch, R. (1958). *Mate selection: A study of complementary needs.* New York: Harper and Row.

Wispe, L. G. (1972). Positive forms of social behaviour: An overview. *Journal of Social Issues, 28*, 1–19.

Wundt, W. (1897). *Outlines of psychology.* New York: Stechert.

Wundt, W. (1916). *Elements of folk psychology: Outlines of a psychological history of the development of mankind.* London: Allen & Unwin.

Zajonc, R. B. (1968). Attitudinal effects of mere exposure. *Journal of Personality & Social Psychology, 9*, 1–27.

Zillman, D. (1979). *Hostility and aggression.* Hillsdale, NJ: Erlbaum.

Zillman, D. (1996). Cognition-excitation interdependencies in aggressive behaviour. *Aggressive Behaviour, 14*, 51–64.